MAKE&MEND

a guide to recycling clothes and fabrics

CUT

SEW loop

HERE X

PRESS

PRESS

DRY CLEAN ONLY

herringbone hem

TACH

12345 seam

backstitch

thread

sew

MEND

fix

60°

stitch

seam

SECTIONS

KNOT

ZIGZAG

make

REVERSE

P

HEM

MAKE&MEND

a guide to recycling clothes and fabrics

By Rebecca Peacock
and Sam Tickner

Spring Hill

Published by Spring Hill, an imprint of How To Books Ltd
Spring Hill House, Spring Hill Road,
Begbroke, Oxford OX5 1RX, United Kingdom
Tel: (01865) 375794. Fax: (01865) 379162
info@howtobooks.co.uk
www.howtobooks.co.uk

First published 2012

How To Books greatly reduce the carbon footprint of their books by sourcing their typesetting and printing in the UK.

British Library Cataloguing in Publication Data.
A catalogue record for this book is available from the British Library.

ISBN: 978-1-905862-79-5

Produced for How To Books by Deer Park Productions, Tavistock, Devon
Designed and typeset by Firecatcher
Printed and bound in Great Britain by Bell & Bain Ltd, Glasgow

NOTE: The material contained in this book is set out in good faith for general guidance and no liability can be accepted
for loss or expense incurred as a result of relying in particular circumstances on statements made in this book. Laws and
regulations are complex and liable to change, and readers should check the current position with the relevant authorities
before making personal arrangements.

CONTENTS

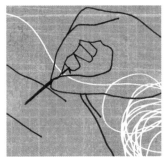

We all know how easy it is to buy a cheap pair of jeans or a couple of low-price T-shirts when our wardrobe becomes rather more shabby than chic. In our fast-paced world, everything, including clothing and soft furnishings for the home, is available at absurdly low prices from the most convenient of places: the supermarket. The need to mend our clothes or keep old fabric to reuse is therefore rather lower on the agenda than it should be. And yet, with the boom and bust of the past decade, as well as issues surrounding the environment, including carbon footprints and unethical trading, these low-cost clothes can be false economy, in terms of the planet, society and your purse.

Mending clothes is a skill that will not only allow your clothes to last longer, but also encourage you to think before you buy. How many times have we groaned to the heavens because our favourite jumper has a hole in it, or we have torn our most comfortable trousers? The ability to get out the sewing kit and restore your treasured clothes to their former glory is invaluable. In addition to this, having the skills to alter clothes will allow you to customise ill-fitting or unsuitable garments into something that will not only fit you perfectly but also be unique to you. It might just be worth buying that £5 dress in the charity shop that is beautiful but doesn't quite fit; a few stitches here and there can work wonders. Even when the repairs aren't worth the effort, there are myriad projects that can be created from scraps of fabric. And, of course, let's not forget the pure joy that comes as a result of saying, 'Yes, I made this myself.'

This book will help you to mend those socks, patch those jeans and customise that T-shirt that has a hole in the front. It will help you to turn old trousers into chic skirts or beloved tops into shopping bags, as well as give you some great ideas for just what to do with that box of scraps. Don't forget to scour the back of the book for stockists and online ideas.

Sorting your clothes

A few weeks ago we moved house and I was forced to look through my rather messy wardrobe. Rather than simply pack everything away I decided to make three piles of clothes. The first contained my wardrobe favourites, those items I loved and always wore. The second, I'm ashamed to say, was larger, and consisted of those clothes that did not fit or were bought with good intentions but never worn. The third consisted of those items of clothes that were torn, stained, worn through or broken. This too was a fairly hefty pile.

I usually go through this rigmarole once a year, and it's surprising how few of the garments I have bought I actually wear. It is surprising, too, that of those I do wear, at least five or six are garments I have altered, recycled or customised. Once I have put away the clothes I love, I then sort the two remaining piles into the following categories.

Clothes that can be repaired or altered

This pile should consist of garments that are structurally fairly sound: those with small tears in seams, holes that can be darned, small stains that can be covered; any item that is too big; trousers that are too short; items with broken zips, or hems that have come down. As a rule, it is worth mending anything that has come apart at a seam. Similarly, if you have any clothes that you don't like because of the pattern or colour, try thinking about whether you might prefer them dyed blue or black, or cut up and turned into a cushion.

Clothes that can be used as fabric

If the garment has a tear that cuts directly into the weave of the fabric, unless it is a treasured possession that can be darned or patched, it is best to sacrifice it to the pile of items you can cut up to turn into something else. If you have any rips in shirts that are not at a seam, or in jeans that are as a result of heavy wear, or any garments that are simply too small or big to bother altering, think about all those lovely things you could make out of them.

Clothes that can be plundered for spares

The garments themselves may be too ripped or small to be used as fabric, but they may be a source of items you can keep for other projects, such as buttons, zips, pockets in jeans, buckles, loops, labels, motifs, ribbons, sequins, beads and so on. It is surprising how useful pockets and buttons from old clothes can be.

Deciding what's worth saving

It is sometimes difficult to weigh up the pros
and cons of mending something. It is helpful
to ask some questions in order to decide if the
garment or item is worth your time and effort.

1. Do you love it? Would you be truly upset if you chopped it up to make
   something else?

2. Is the tear or rip on a seam? If you sew the seam back together, will this
   solve the problem?

3. If the item is stained, can it be patched without ruining the design?
   Could it be dyed a suitably dark colour to cover the stain?

4. If the garment is too big, will a small alteration solve the problem?

5. If it is too small, can you find suitable fabric to enlarge it?

If you answer yes to these questions, then it is a good idea to get your
mending box out. If no, then the recycling box will have a happy addition.

Recycling clothes and fabric

With the current worries about climate change and our economic problems, recycling our waste is something we are all familiar with. The benefits of both reducing waste and the need to use more raw materials are well documented. However, the notion of recycling clothes seems to be confined to donating a bag to a charity shop, or pushing our tatty old bits and bobs into the clothing bank.

Recycling our clothes should be something we do for ourselves. Making synthetic fibres uses energy and natural resources, as they are derived from petrochemicals. If we consider the impact on the environment of each stage of producing a garment, the price tag to the consumer may be low, but the cost to the planet seems vastly out of proportion to such benefits. Consider the many hidden problems, from the impact of intensive farming of cotton, to the chemicals used in the dyeing and printing processes, right through to social issues arising from the conditions for workers in factories. Similarly the energy consumed and the carbon released in the delivery of cheap, synthetic clothing from the Far East to the UK is at huge cost to the planet. Consequently, now the clothes are here, it would be a shame if they are not used until they disintegrate.

There are a number of benefits to be derived from reusing and recycling our fabrics. Not only are we, in however small a way, reducing the demand for new items, neither are we using up space in a landfill (where synthetic fabrics can linger for up to 40 years). In addition, we are saving ourselves money. It is fairly easy to work this out precisely.

If a garment costs £30 to buy new, and you wear it ten times, the price per wear is £3. If the garment then gets a hole in it and you throw it away, you have to spend another £30 to replace it. However, if you repair the garment, you can wear it again and again. If you wear it a further five times, the price per wear is now £2, and you haven't had to fork out for a new one. The more you wear it, the more money you save!

Similarly, if your item is not suitable for repair, but can be turned into something else, that item can fill a hole in your wardrobe that would have been filled by a £20 bag or a £15 scarf. See? Makes sense, doesn't it?

RECYCLE!

snazzy shorts

bag →

mini skirt

Storing items for recycling

If you really can't mend an item, then it can quite easily be successfully dismantled for future use. If you can spare a section of your wardrobe for items you will later recycle, that's fine. Alternatively, a small set of plastic drawers, available from hardware shops for around £10–£15, is ideal, provided everything is stored safely and wisely.

Dismantling garments

To retain the maximum amount of fabric from a garment, a seam ripper is a must. It will allow you to cut through the seams, preserving the fabric right to the edge, in half the time it takes to pick through the stitches with scissors. This is useful, too, as it allows you to deconstruct the garment and create patterns from it for future use.

Trousers/shorts

Turn inside out and unpick the seams on the inside legs. Using a seam ripper, unpick the rear and front seams right up to the waistband, allowing you two large pieces. Wash, press and fold carefully. Remove all buttons and zips carefully and store for future use. Cut off the rear pockets of jeans by sliding the unpicker underneath the patch.

Fitted skirts

Remove all buttons and zips. If the skirt is lined, remove the lining at the waistband and cut through seams to provide 2–3 pieces. Unpick the side seams of the skirt, providing you with 2–3 pieces. Wash, press and fold carefully.

Flared skirts

Cut off the waistband and cut down the seams. Wash, press and fold carefully.

Shirts

Remove all buttons, cut off the collar and cuffs. Unpick the seam holding the sleeves on. Unpick all remaining seams. Wash, press and fold carefully.

T-shirts

Leave as they are; simply wash and roll them up to store.

Woollen jumpers

Turn inside out, lie flat and cut off the side seams and sleeves. To avoid the knit unravelling, fold some wide, low-tack masking tape (available from most DIY shops) along the edges and stick down.

Cardigans

Remove all buttons/embellishments. Turn inside out, cut off sleeves and open them along the inside seam. Cut off cuffs if necessary. Cut along the side seams of the cardigan and cover edges with masking tape if necessary.

Coats

Remove all fastenings, zips, buttons, etc. Turn inside out and remove any lining with an unpicker. If the coat is lined with wadding, remove this for future use. Otherwise, unpick all major seams and press each piece flat.

Storing your equipment

If you wish to make recycling and reusing fabrics a permanent pastime, it is useful to invest in a couple of shelves to house your collected buttons, zips and equipment. Vintage tins and jars can make your storage area look particularly attractive; second-hand shops and Internet auction sites are useful sources for these. Colour coding buttons not only makes them look pretty, but also makes them easier to find.

Old wooden spice racks are lovely for storing your cotton spools, or why not make your own spool holder, following the instructions given here?

SPOOL HOLDER

You will need

An old picture frame, preferably with a wooden back (If it doesn't have one, have a piece of MDF cut to fit inside it)

A metal rule

Some 5cm (2in) nails

Panel pins for securing the back board

To make

1. Measure the diameter of your largest spool and add 5mm to the measurement.

2. Make sure the back board of the frame is securely fixed to it (you may need to knock a few panel pins into the back to keep it safe). Calculate the area of the inside of the frame by multiplying the length by the width.

3. Divide up the inside of the frame into squares using a rule. Your aim is to create squares that are big enough to house the largest of your spools. To do this, you will need to divide the area by the figure you obtained at step 1 (the diameter of your largest spool plus 5mm) to give you the number of squares.

4. Find the middle of each square. This is where you will place each nail.

5. Knock the nails into the back board gently, to ensure they don't come too far out of the back. Two to three hits should do the trick.

6. Once all the nails are in place, you can paint the frame. When it is dry, put your spools in place and admire your handiwork!

Storing your fabric

For smaller pieces of fabric (i.e. under 300 x 200mm), plastic paper wallets and a sturdy A4 lever arch file will make your swatches easy to find as well as keeping them flat and dry. It is useful to divide them into colours and patterns to make finding them again easy.

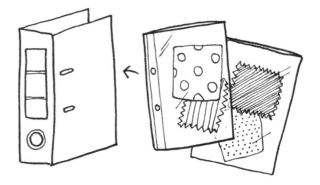

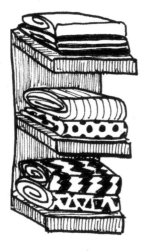

Square CD racks with shelves that hold 10 to 15 CDs are a great way of storing fat quarters of fabric. These are cuts of cloth that are usually a quarter of a yard or metre in area. They are great for patchwork or smaller projects, such as bags or jewellery. Simply fold them up and place on the shelf. Keeping like colours to a single square will make this look as attractive as possible.

Larger pieces of fabric can be either folded and kept in a drawer, or rolled together and stored in postal tubes. If you cut a small section from the corner of each and tape it to the outside of the tube, you will quickly and easily find what you are looking for. Postal tubes will keep the fabric dry and away from moths, should you have any natural fibres amongst your stores. Vacuum-seal bags are also a great way of storing fabric, as all the air is removed from the bag, thus reducing its volume. Store these under the bed or in a cupboard and they'll keep your fabric dry and safe, as well as out of sight.

Where to go for inspiration and materials

To a frugal craftsperson, the recycled wardrobe is but the first port of call for sources of inspiration and materials. Charity and second-hand shops are fantastic for finding interesting patterns, textures and designs that can be chopped up for your own gain. Try looking for clothes with unusual buttons, excessive beading and bright colours. (Don't forget to wash everything you buy, just in case.)

It is worth using the Internet to find local factory shops that sell fabric seconds. Some textile factories have excess stock or offcuts that can be bought for under a pound. It is worth telephoning to ask about their policy on donating offcuts, or to see if they will give you any small free samples, which are great for patchworking.

The Internet itself is another great place for finding freebies. Sites such as Twitter and Facebook allow you to connect with like-minded people, providing you with a platform for sharing your work, finding inspiration and also asking cheeky questions, such as: 'Anyone have any spare bits of fabric they no longer want?' It's good practice in cases such as this to send a stamped addressed envelope to the donor, or to make a little something and send it back as a thank you.

I cannot lie. There have been times in my 20 years of sewing when I have wanted to throw whatever twisted, torn piece of fabric I had been working on across the room in a fit of frustration. I have broken hundreds of needles, I have busted zips, and ruined yards of cloth. I have even burned huge holes in acrylic fabric by using an iron on the wrong setting. There is a very good reason for this: it is because I have, in the past, been somewhat impatient.

Patience is more than a virtue in sewing; it is imperative. Without it, the many stages of creating something that looks as good as possible will be painfully difficult. It may sound all too obvious, but having the patience to observe all the steps in a project will not only make it easier to create, but also ensure that your product looks the best it can and lasts as long as possible. For proof of this we need only inspect examples of delicate hand-sewn work that has survived for hundreds of years, created by patient ladies who made each of their stitches as uniform as possible. When we compare it with the rushed, cheap, machined work available today from supermarkets around the world, it is clear that patience adds a certain longevity.

As with most things, a good grounding in the basic techniques of sewing will stand you in excellent stead for creating functional and beautiful items. Most of the equipment you will require for general darning, mending and repair work is available at your local supermarket. However, for more ambitious projects, or simply to have a wider arsenal against repair tasks that may crop up, you may want some more specialist equipment. The following information includes everything you will need, short of going into business as a seamstress.

Are you sitting comfortably?

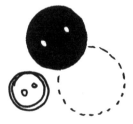

Needles

Even this most basic piece of equipment can be a bit of a minefield. When faced with a wall of packets in the haberdashery and the question 'What type of needles?' from the assistant, the temptation to run away can be great. However, identifying the right type of needle for your job can result in an easier project and fewer cases of sewing fury.

Self-threading

If only this were so! These needles can sometimes be more trouble than they are worth, though some people swear by them. They have a fine slot at the end of the eye, through which the thread is forced. Beware, though: finer or poor-quality threads have a habit of breaking in this process.

Crewel

These are general sewing needles – very sharp, with a round eye and medium in length. These needles can be used for most jobs.

Embroidery

These are very similar to crewel (and are sometimes sold as embroidery crewels), being sharp and medium in length. They do, however, have a much larger eye to accommodate multiple strands of embroidery thread and are therefore a good starting point for a beginner.

Beading

These are long, extremely fine needles used for decorative bead work. They are invaluable for use with seed beads, as crewel or embroidery needles can sometimes be too thick, and your bead can become stuck on the eye.

Quilting

Short needles with sharp points and small eyes, these are used for small stitches on thicker fabrics, such as wool, denim, or the many layers of quilting.

Tapestry

These are thick needles with a very long eye (to accommodate wool) and a blunt tip to prevent damaging tapestry fabrics when sewing. They are not good for common repair jobs.

Chenille

These are larger needles with long eyes and a sharp tip for getting through closely woven fabric. They are good for doing basic repairs on thick fabrics. Don't use them on leather or plastics as, owing to their thickness, they may leave a hole.

Darning

These are similar to tapestry needles, as they are blunt, but are much longer. They are great for passing between threads in jobs that require a darn.

NEEDLES

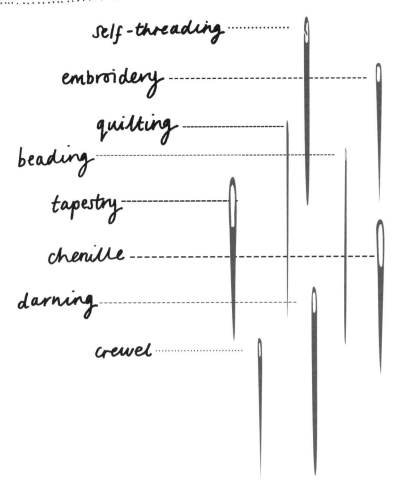

self-threading

embroidery

quilting

beading

tapestry

chenille

darning

crewel

Choosing the right needle for the job

Tears in thin, delicate fabrics	Crewel needle
Tears in thick, open-weave fabrics	Darning needle
Tears in thick, fine-weave fabrics	Chenille needle
Holes in socks, jumpers, etc.	Darning needle
Seam rips in thin fabrics	Crewel needle
Seam rips in thick fabrics	Chenille needle
Patching thin fabrics	Crewel needle
Patching thick fabrics	Chenille needle

Pins

There are a variety of pins available to cater
for every type of fabric. As a rule, a basic set
of standard pins (with coloured ball heads) will
suit you very nicely for most jobs. However,
if you have very delicate fabric, you will need
some lace pins, which will not leave large holes
after they have been removed. A stock of
safety pins is also useful for quick repair jobs.

Cutting tools

Scissors

A good pair of scissors is as essential to a sewing job as the fabric itself. Ideally, they
are made of high-grade steel and have an adjustable screw to allow an even pressure,
no matter what the fabric. It is advisable to buy a pair of dressmaker's scissors, and to
spend as much as you can afford, as this will make your future projects so much neater
and easier to deal with. It is best to use your scissors only for cutting fabric; if you use
them for cutting paper, flowers or for general family use, you will ruin the blade.

Pinking shears

A pair of pinking shears will also be useful as they create edges that will not fray. They
are also used to create decorative edges and work especially well with felt. They have
heavy, zigzag blades.

Embroidery scissors

These will allow you to snip the ends of thread neatly, and they also help in cutting the
stitches of seams if your seam ripper is proving difficult. They have sharp, pointed
blades and are roughly half the size of dressmaker's scissors.

Seam ripper

This is an invaluable tool for undoing seams, removing stitches and buttonholes.
Comprising of a hooked blade with a handle, the tip is placed under stitches and pushed
forward, cutting the thread.

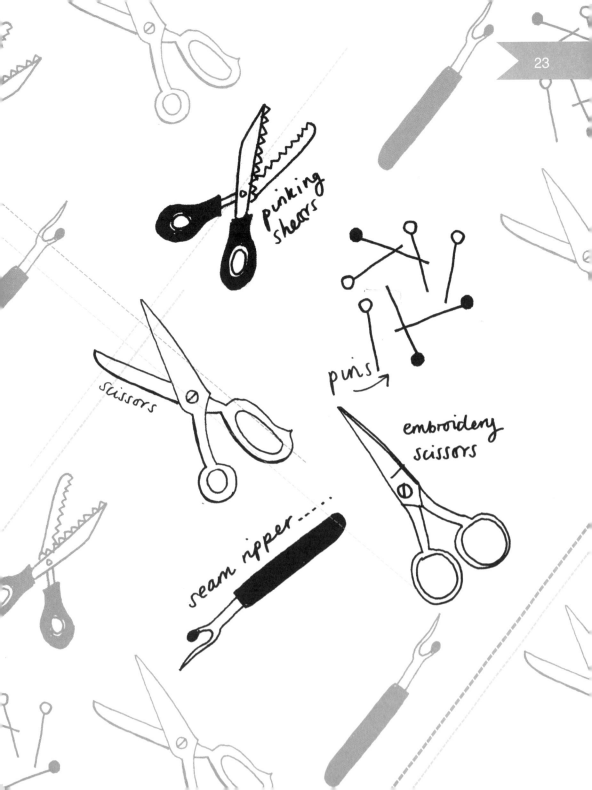

pinking shears

pins →

scissors

embroidery scissors

seam ripper----

Other tools

Tape measure

The tailor's favourite, a must for all sewing kits, this will see you through many years. A retractable one will make rolling it up a bit easier, but is not essential.

Chalk

Making things from scratch will usually result in your needing to draw out shapes on fabric. Tailor's chalk allows you to transfer the pattern shape onto the fabric without creating a lasting stain. It is available as a block or as pens. The marks disappear after 48 hours.

Thimble

This is a small shield used on the index finger to protect it from being pricked by the needle. To be honest, I never use one, but many people swear by them. They usually come in sewing packs, so are worth a try, just in case you find them useful.

Pincushion

Another time-saving bit of kit that really does help, this allows you to store and reuse pins quickly while you are working. Pincushions come in a variety of guises, and their designs can be quite creative, as you can see from the cute little hedgehog to the right. You can find out how to make one just like it by turning to page 26...

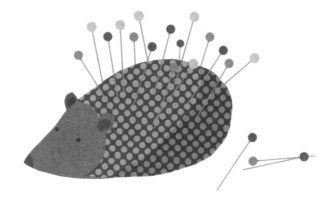

Point turner

This allows you to flatten out seams and darts, as well as turn smaller items the right way out after sewing inside seams. I have often used a wide-tooth comb just as successfully for this.

Darning mushroom

A lovely piece of equipment, this allows you to spread out the item that needs darning and view the work easily.

Dressmaker's dummy

This is a dream product, but expensive, and only worth getting if you are serious about sewing (in other words, you will make many full garments for different people). They are available in different sizes, usually with adjustable elements to accommodate three to four dress sizes, and enable you to test the fit of a garment, or make small adjustments, as well as see what your garment will look like.

Iron and ironing board

These really are essential pieces of equipment. Each piece of fabric should be pressed before use, as any creases in the fabric may alter the shape of your finished item. Pressed seams are also much easier to sew and look so much neater and more professional. Travel irons work well and are smaller to store. A thick towel on a firm surface will work in place of an ironing board if space is an issue.

Pressing cloth

This is necessary when working with delicate fabrics, and stops any unnecessary accidents, such as melting fabrics or making shiny marks.

Embroidery ring

This consists of two plastic or wooden rings, affixed using an adjustable screw, which holds your fabric taut as you embroider it. Embroidery rings come in a range of sizes and are an invaluable addition to the sewing kit. Ideally, you should purchase a small, medium and large version for all your needs, though a medium-sized one will probably see you through the majority of tasks.

HEDGEHOG PINCUSHION

There are a couple of variations with this project; you can use a different colour fabric for the face, which does make it a little trickier, but gives the hedgehog a lot more character. Thick fabrics work best with this project: tweed, denim, mock suede and heavy cotton are all good. If you do want to use thinner fabric, iron on some interfacing in a medium stiffness to give it a bit more resilience. For the stuffing, you can use anything suitable, such as wool, polyester stuffing or the contents of an old pillow. The denser the stuffing, the better the pins will adhere to the cushion.

You will need

A piece of thick fabric 300 x 300mm for the upper body

A piece of thick fabric 250 x 250mm for the base

A piece of medium weight interfacing 250 x 250mm

A large handful of stuffing

A button or bead for the nose

2 buttons or beads for the eyes

A piece of dark felt 30 x 60mm for the ears

If you wish to use a lighter fabric for the face, you'll need 100 x 150mm of a contrasting, thick fabric.

To make

1. Iron the medium weight interfacing to your chosen base fabric. This will ensure your hedgehog keeps its shape.

2. Cut one base and two side pieces from your chosen fabrics. Pin the two side pieces together, reverse sides out, and sew along the top seam. This will join the sides to form the main body.

3. Pin the body to the base, keeping the edges together. Sew all round, except for a 4cm gap at the back.

4. Turn the hedgehog inside out and fill tightly with your chosen stuffing.

5. Now for the tricky part: pull the hole closed and fold the frayed edges inside so that they can't be seen. Pin this in place.

6. Using a thread that blends in as closely as possible with your fabric, oversew the hole closed. The main body of your hedgehog is now complete.

7. Sew a chunky button or bead onto the tip of the nose, and add two smaller ones for the eyes.

8. Glue or sew the ears in place.

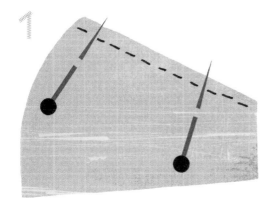

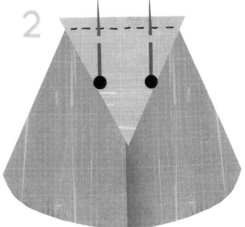

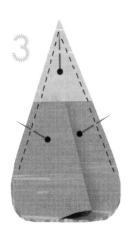

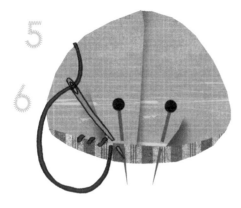

embroidery ring

point turner

iron

dressmakers dummy

pressing cloth

darning mushroom NOT →

Thread

A good haberdashery will bombard you with a wall of thread in myriad colours, thicknesses and weights. It is important to navigate this section carefully, as not only can the wrong thread distort your work (if too heavy), leave unsightly holes (if too thick), or break upon the first use, but scrimping on the quality can knot up the thread and frustrate you to the point where you never want to sew again. As with needles, the choice of thread should be dictated by your choice of fabric. Silk fabrics should be sewn with a silk thread, cotton with cotton, etc. Man-made fabrics should be matched with a polyester thread of similar weight.

However, it is possible to get good results from cheap polyester thread that is available widely. If your fabric is thick, double up the thread to ensure your sewing will stand up to harder wear.

Tacking thread

This cotton thread is great for temporary seams to be finished later after fitting. It can be easily unpicked and is not strong enough for permanent work.

Cotton thread

A good all-round thread for hand or machine stitching. The cotton is treated using a process called Mercerisation, in which the thread is treated with sodium hydroxide to create a stronger yarn with a lustrous appearance.

Polyester thread

The most common, widely available thread that can be used on most fabrics. It is favoured for its strength and suits synthetic fabrics perfectly.

Stranded cotton

This is sold in skeins rather than on bobbins and consists of six fine strands which are separated for use in embroidery and needlepoint. It is great for any decorative stitches and comes in a whole rainbow of colours.

Silk thread

A fine, delicate, yet strong thread for use with natural fabric, such as wool and silk. Used especially by those genius tailors on Savile Row.

Tapestry wool

Mainly used for making tapestry designs, this thick wool is also used to edge blankets or for any decorative edging on heavyweight fabrics.

Fabrics

When you are repairing clothes it is not always possible to know exactly what type of fabric you are using. It is useful if you do know, however, as fabrics behave in different ways. The main types are as follows.

Cottons

Humans have been using cotton fabrics for millennia, thanks to its versatility, strength and comfort. The versatility of the fibres means it can be produced in a range of weights, from lighter fabrics such as gingham, seersucker and lawn, to thick corduroy and velvets. Cotton can be easily blended with other fibres such as silk or polyester to produce delicate or easy care fabrics.

Gingham

A lightweight fabric with an even check, this is commonly seen on farmhouse tables or as school dresses. Wash at 60°/use a hot iron.

Chintz

Somewhat unfashionable now, this closely woven fabric with a glaze is used for sofas, curtains and the odd dress. It is hard wearing and particularly dirt resistant, thanks to the glaze. Dry clean only/use a warm iron on reverse.

Seersucker

A lightweight fabric with a puckered check running through it, this is used most commonly for shirts and children's clothes. Wash at 60°/ needs no ironing.

Lawn

Plain, smooth and absorbent, this is frequently used for baby clothes or any other softer item. Wash at 40°/use a warm iron.

Muslin

This inexpensive, multifunctional fabric can be used as interlining, window dressing or as test fabric for difficult jobs. It is also used in the making of cheeses and jams, though best not sew with it afterwards. Wash at 40°/use a cool iron.

Voile

A sheer fabric frequently used for windows, thin blouses and dresses. It can be notoriously difficult to machine stitch, so make sure you choose the correct needles and thread. Wash at 40°/use a cool iron.

Broderie anglaise

Usually made as a cotton/synthetic mix, this fabric has decorative eyelets embroidered within it and is frequently used for table linen, bedding and nightwear. Wash at 60°/use a warm iron on reverse.

Linen

Derived from fibres from the flax plant, linen is a luxury fabric that is frequently blended with silk for a softer feel. Linen is breathable and therefore excellent for clothing, especially in warm climates, though it is notorious for its tendency to crease.

Suit linen

A strong fabric, frequently used for suits and outerwear. It creases easily, so care should be taken in the storage of linen clothes. Hand wash only/use a hot iron with a damp cloth on the wrong side.

Handkerchief linen

A finer linen, used for lingerie, blouses and bedding. It has a plain weave and drapes nicely, unlike suit linen, due to its lighter nature. Wash at 40°/use a warm iron with a damp cloth on the wrong side.

Synthetic fabrics

These fabrics are developed from petrochemicals and plant cellulose (rayon fabrics), and are on the whole durable, crease resistant and not prone to insect attack. However, synthetic fabrics are not 'breathable' or hugely absorbent. They are frequently combined with natural fibres to improve their texture and durability, while making them cost-effective and machine washable. Some synthetic fabrics are not good under an iron, so be sure to check the label.

Acrylic

A lightweight fabric that is coloured before it is made into fibres, acrylic has a warm, woollen feel. It is often used as an inexpensive alternative to cashmere due to the softness of the fibres. Wash at 40°/ use a warm iron.

Microfibre

A durable, waterproof fabric with an extremely dense weave made from polyester. This is now used in most types of clothing. Wash at 40°/use a cool iron on the wrong side.

Petticoat net

A nylon fabric that can be quite abrasive next to the skin, this is usually used for costumes, petticoats and ballet skirts. Hand wash only/ use a cool iron.

Viscose

Made from plant pulp dissolved in caustic soda, viscose is a strong, soft and absorbent fabric that is often used for dresses and skirts. Wash at 40°/use a warm iron while damp.

Wool

Wool is a natural animal fibre that comes from sheep, alpaca, goats and Angora rabbits. It is not only durable, but comfortable, water resistant and versatile. Like cotton, it can be mixed with synthetic fabrics to create extremely comfortable, flame retardant, washable materials. However, wool is prone to damage from moths and heat, so some washing and ironing rules need to be followed. It is a good idea to invest in a pressing cloth to avoid wool becoming shiny when ironed, and avoid using a sweeping motion to ensure garments don't become misshapen.

Flannel

Commonly used for suits and jackets, this strong fabric has a plain weave and matt finish. It is fairly thick and warm, and works well in formal attire. Hand wash or dry-clean only/use warm iron on the wrong side.

Tartan

All jokes about Scotsmen's kilts aside, tartan is a twill weave fabric that is carefully woven into patterns. It frays easily, so raw edges should be cut with pinking shears. Dry-clean only/use a warm iron on the wrong side.

Jersey

This can also be made from cotton (commonly T-shirt material). Woollen single jersey is used for sportswear as it is elastic and breathable, though double jersey is firmer, bulky and used mainly for suits. Wash at 40°/use a hot iron with a damp cloth.

Cashmere

A fine, expensive, luxurious fabric that is noted for its softness and warmth. It is usually made into cardigans and coats. Hand wash or dry-clean only/do not iron.

Tweed

A firm favourite of mine, tweed is a thick woven fabric that is produced in a range of patterns and colours. Traditional tweeds, such as Harris Tweed from the Hebrides, are dyed using local natural dyes. Dry-clean only/use a warm iron with a damp cloth.

Mohair

A specialist fabric made with angora wool, which has a hairy texture, usually mixed with sheep's wool. It is used mainly for ladies' clothes and outerwear. Dry-clean only/use a warm iron with a damp cloth.

Silk

A much sought after fabric, created from the very fine, soft fibre produced by the larvae of silkworms to make their cocoons, silk has a triangular structure, allowing light to reflect from its surface and give a lustrous appearance. It is one of the strongest natural fibres, though it has little elasticity; and, like wool, it is prone to shrinkage and attack from insects. When you are sewing with silk it is best to check on a sample piece of fabric whether needles and pins will leave a permanent hole. If you do not have fine enough pins, make sure you pin the fabric within the seam allowance to avoid damaging your garment.

Silk and wool mix

Found most commonly in expensive suits, the wool adds body and softness to the lustre of the silk. This fabric drapes nicely and is best suited to quality tailoring. Dry-clean only/use a warm iron on the wrong side.

Silk and cotton mix

A luxurious lightweight fabric used for delicate clothes, this has the sheen and drape of silk with the weave of cotton for strength and structure. Wash at 40°/use a warm iron on the wrong side.

Silk satin

A fabric with a strong sheen, this is used for a range of luxury items, such as evening wear, dresses and accessories. Wash at 40°/use a warm iron without steam on the wrong side, using a cloth.

Taffeta

Named from the Persian for 'twisted woven', this firm, smooth fabric has a strong sheen and is used mainly for evening or formal wear, curtains and even wall coverings. Dry-clean only/use a warm iron without steam on the wrong side.

Organza

This is a sheer fabric traditionally created from Chinese silk, though it is now more commonly sold as viscose or acetate organza. Hand wash or dry-clean only/use a cool iron.

Chiffon

Another sheer, open-weave fabric made from crepe (high-twist) yarns, used for evening wear and blouses. As the fabric frays easily, hems should be double folded to prevent the threads showing. Wash at 40°/use a cool iron without steam.

Underlying fabrics

These fabrics are used to give bulk, provide warmth, comfort, or simply to hide the raw edges and messy seams that occur in the manufacture of garments. They are usually made from synthetic fibres and can be easily purchased from any haberdashery or craft store.

Linings

Usually have a soft, silky finish and are used in jackets, some fitted skirts and luxury bags. You can buy silk, polyester, jersey, rayon, or satin lining, though any thin fabric can be recycled as a lining.

Wadding

Polyester wadding allows you to add bulk to projects such as quilts, padded bags and toys. It is available in a wide range of weights and thicknesses, and can be recycled from many different products.

Interfacing

Non-woven or woven, iron-on or sew-in, light, medium or heavy weight, there is an interfacing for every job. For most projects, I opt for a medium weight iron-on interfacing, though waistbands and heavyweight fabrics will require a heavier interfacing. If in doubt, match the fabric weight to the interfacing. Interfacing is also a great way of modifying the weight of a fabric, enabling you to use an old T-shirt for a structured bag. If you do this, make sure you choose a white interfacing for light colours and a black one for darker examples. Interfacing is an excellent way of keeping embroidered fabrics taut and neat, so try using a lightweight version when making motifs or monograms.

Notions

These are the bits and bobs you may need along the way to complete certain projects. They can get a little confusing, so we shall stick to the most common ones.

Buckles

Everyone is familiar with buckles, having used them from an early age. Buckles are available to buy online or from your trusty haberdashery. They are usually ready made, but can also be bought in kit form, allowing you to cover the buckle with fabric. In each case, they are attached to garments by creating a fabric loop which is then stitched closed to keep the buckle in place.

buckles →

D rings

These are an inexpensive addition to the sewing box that will make your bags so much sturdier and look much more professional. They are usually D-shaped or circular pieces of steel or plastic that are attached to bags via fabric loops. Handles are then attached to the ring, providing a stronger link between the bag and any straps. D rings can be purchased from any haberdashery or leathercraft supplier, or can be salvaged from old bags.

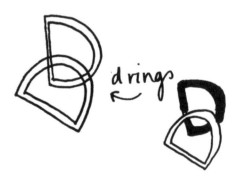

d rings

Bindings

Very handy for making a strong seam, bindings are also fantastic for neatening raw edges of fabric. Wider bindings can be folded over raw edges and sewn in place for a neat, sturdy finish. Iron-on bindings are exceptionally useful for finishing trouser hems before sewing over for a secure finish.

binding.

Ribbons

There is something so lovely about seeing spools and spools of ribbon lined up for sale. I have to admit to spending hours in this section of the haberdashery as ribbons tend to hypnotise me. In practical terms, ribbon is an easy, cheap and decorative way to finish your hems, create straps for bags and tops or cover tears. There is a wide variety on the market, including the most common single or double-faced satin, woven metallic, woven jacquard grosgrain, wire edged (great for making bows), gingham and the deliciously festive velvet. I usually try and keep a store of ribbon in large Kilner jars to keep it dust free. They also make an attractive addition to any shelf. A ribbon store is useful as a quick gift wrapping facility when certain special days have been overlooked.

Elastics

An extremely useful product, elastic is fabric or tape containing interwoven strands of flexible rubber or a similar substance that allow it to stretch and return to its former shape. It is used for waistbands, in lingerie and in sportswear as a quick, comfortable alternative to zips, belts and buttons. There is a wide variety of elastic on the market, which is bought for colour, width, pattern or thickness. It is useful to keep a supply of it in the sewing kit for quick alterations or amendments.

Decorative trims

The options are almost endless for the range of decorative trims on the market. From delicate lace, to feather edging, to braids, there is something out there for every project. Trims are either inserted in hems or stitched to the fabric surface. Trims that are flatter, such as those made of lace or broderie anglaise, can be sewn in using a machine, though bulkier or decorative items such as feather edging or sequin strips should be stitched by hand.

Beads

I have pots and pots of tiny seed beads rolling around in my sewing kit, mainly because they look absolutely lovely together, but also as they are a fantastic way of making beautiful decorative motifs or patterns. Ensure you invest in a pack of beading needles, as most crewel or self-threading needles will not pass through the smaller examples, and some will break them in half.

Patches

Those legendary brown suede patches on the elbows of tweed jackets are a must if you are an esteemed academic or Stephen Fry, but are also an extremely easy way of covering wear and tear. Suede patches are usually bought with pre-punched holes to help you to get through the thick fabric with a standard needle, as well as create a neat stitching line. Cloth patches do the same trick, though they can leave a garment looking as if either a scout has attacked it or you have just been initiated into a biker gang. If you do not fit into either of these categories, try a spot of lace instead.

Shoulder pads

These 1980s mainstays are enjoying a resurgence in popularity. They are made of soft wadding placed between layers of interfacing or thin felt material. If they are to your taste, simply hand sew them in place before applying lining to your jacket, or after you have inserted sleeves in shirts.

Braids and fringes

Frequently seen on the edges of sofas or brocade cushions, braids and fringes provide a decorative touch, while covering a multitude of sins. Narrow braids are frequently used in couture fashion (particularly by Chanel) to finish skirts and jackets, or on curtains to fringe tops and bottoms. They usually need to be sewn on by hand, so make sure you have good strong chenille needles ready for a marathon curtain sewing session.

Zips

As with ribbons, a zip stanchion in a shop can leave you somewhat hypnotised by the myriad colours, lengths and types available. The basic types are as follows.

Metallic

Most commonly seen in jeans, the metallic zip is constructed from individual teeth set on tape at regular intervals, usually made from nickel. The zip is closed using a metal zip slider that hooks the teeth together. Metallic zips are generally very strong and reliable. A polyester version of this zip is also popular.

Coil

A coil of polyester wire on each side of the tape makes up the teeth of this popular zip, with a metal or polyester slider to keep it closed, and a closed base. Coil zips are extremely common in all types of clothing and bags, and come in a wide range of colours.

Concealed

Used mainly in fashion, this type of zip has its teeth behind the tape, making it invisible. It is constructed from a polyester coil and is closed at the base.

Open-ended

These zips are usually made of polyester and can be completely unzipped into two halves, for use in jackets or coats. They have a 'box and pin' mechanism to lock them in place when closed.

The sewing machine

A source of wonder and bemusement for many, the sewing machine is a wonderful item that allows you to produce high-quality, sturdy items in a fraction of the time it takes to sew by hand. There are hundreds of machines out there, from all-singing, all-dancing computerised numbers that could probably walk your dog and make your breakfast for you, to the miniature versions available from supermarkets.   The options are alarmingly vast. However, the best sewing machine for you is one that offers at least:

* straight stitch
* zigzag stitch
* buttonhole stitch
* stitch length change function
* stitch width change function

If the best machine you can afford has these functions then you will be able to complete the vast majority of projects with ease. Many of the other decorative stitches are usually just a bonus.

How a sewing machine works

The sewing machine is constructed around a simple but ingenious idea: the lock stitch. This stitch is quite different from the way we would ordinarily hand sew fabric together, as it relies on two separate threads working together to lock the thread and create a strong, neat seam.

Top thread

The top thread forms the visible part of the stitch, and is housed on top of the machine. The thread passes through a number of items, detailed below.

1. The upper thread guide: this is a small loop on the top of the machine that keeps your thread on the right road.
2. Tension discs: the thread passes through a number of invisible mechanisms that regulate the tension of the thread. They set the amount of thread that is available for each stitch. If the tension is too tight, there is not enough thread passed through for the stitch. If the tension is too loose, there is an excess of thread passed through, resulting in loopy, loose stitches. This mechanism usually forces your thread down, then up, then down again.
3. The lower thread guide: this is housed above the needle and allows the thread to remain in place before going through the needle. You'll find the machine will not work without the thread in the correct position.
4. The needle: this is placed in an adjustable clamp, allowing you to remove and change the needle according to the fabric type. As with hand stitching, it is important to ensure that the needle is the correct one for the job in hand (see page 42).

SEWING MACHINE of GLORY

Dont forget to give him a name

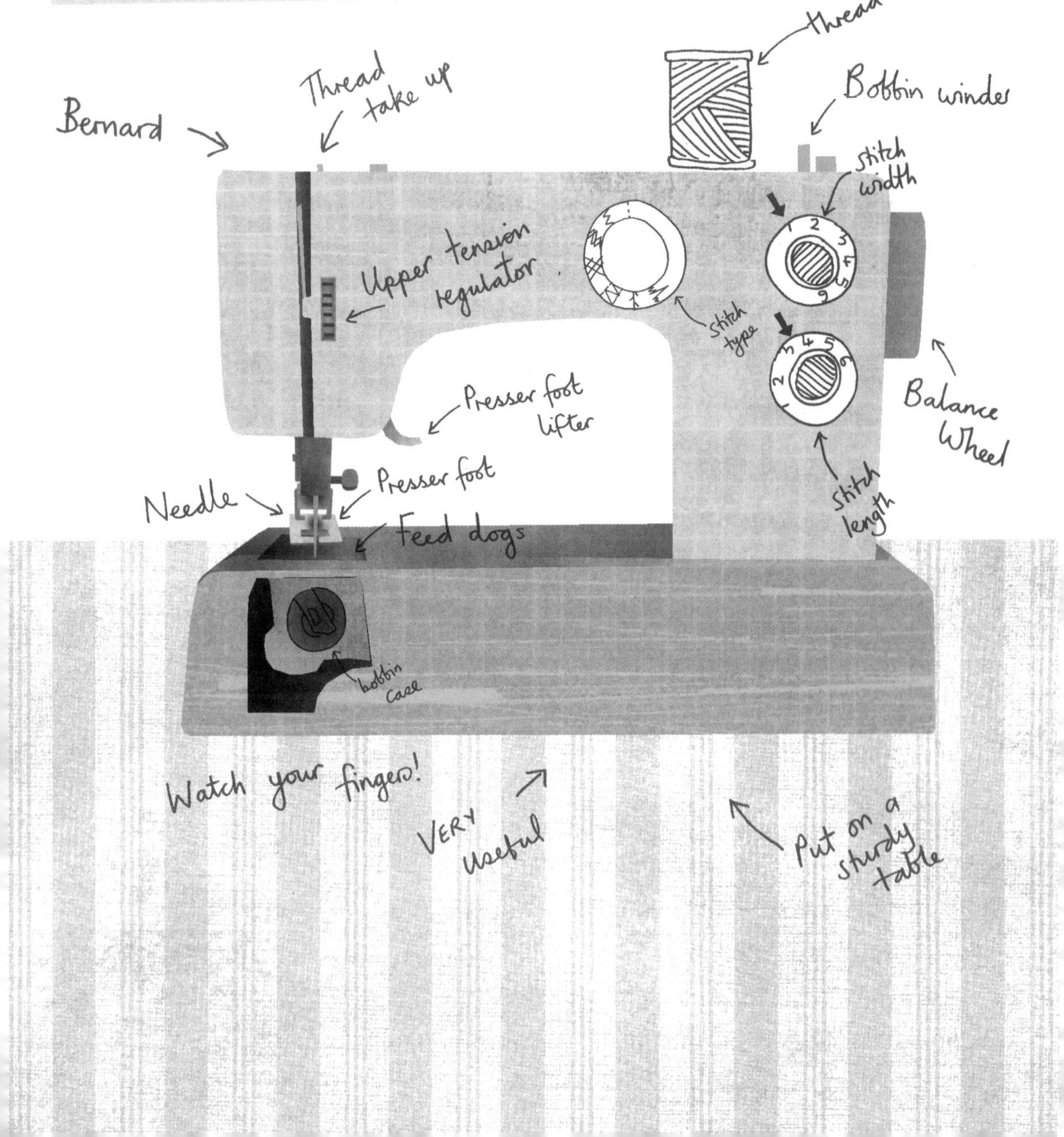

Lower thread

The lower thread is housed within a bobbin or spool case, which is then placed inside the lower section of the sewing machine. The bobbin case has a screw which can be altered to achieve the correct tension. This can be a little tiresome, if you forget to alter the tension for your next job. It is best to keep a couple of bobbin cases, with one kept permanently altered for infrequently used threads that require a firmer tension.

How a stitch is made

The bobbin is placed within a shuttle, which is turned by the motor of the sewing machine in synchronisation with the needle above. The upper thread is forced through the fabric and through a hole in the shuttle. The thread is then caught by the shuttle hook and pulled around the lower thread, forming a locked stitch. The fabric is pulled along by the feed dogs, just enough for the next stitch to be made.

The presser foot

The fabric is placed on the metal plate and held in place by the presser foot. This can be adjusted and changed, depending on the job in hand.

There is a large number of presser feet available, with a few of the more common ones usually packaged as part of your machine. The purpose of all of them is to make it much easier to sew difficult things such as zips and buttons. A general foot will see you through most of the projects in this book, though a zip foot does make adding those tricky fasteners so much easier.

Needles

Just as for hand sewing, there is a wide range of needles available for different fabrics and requirements, and you should take into consideration the fabric type before beginning. The rule for needles is:

- finer needles for fine fabrics
- ballpoint needles for knits
- sharp-point needles for woven fabrics
- denim needle for thick fabrics and denims

It is best to purchase a pack of general sharp needles as these will suit you for the majority of projects in this book.

Understanding tension

The main difficulty with the sewing machine usually stems from the problem of tension. However, the tension dials are not difficult to master once you understand what they do.

We have already touched on the tension discs on the upper thread. You will find a small dial near this area of the machine, usually containing numbers from 1 to 9. This gauge will adjust your upper tension and alter the amount of thread allowed through for each stitch.

To adjust your tension, place a sample of the fabric you are going to sew under the needle, drop the foot and sew a straight line.

If the stitches look even, your tension is fine.

If the stitches look tight, with the underside thread peeping through, the tension is too tight. Reduce it by one and try again. Repeat until the stitches look secure.

If the stitches are slightly loopy and look too loose, the tension is too low. Increase it by one and repeat until the stitches look secure.

Decorative and unusual threads

The tension on the sewing machine will be altered by factors such as whether or not the thread is elastic or metallic. Elastic threads create their own tension, so reduce the tension on your machine to account for this. Metallic threads also require a lower tension, as they are usually slightly stretchy, as do thicker threads. Again, a test patch is best to ensure your stitches will do the job.

Bobbin case tension

Your bobbin case tension should, as a rule, be set for the majority of jobs. If you are using a particularly thick thread, it may be necessary to lower the bobbin thread tension slightly, and in such cases this should be done on a separate bobbin case, as it is difficult to reset.

trouble shooting...

The sewing machine can sometimes be a temperamental little beast. It is best to make sure, before you begin sewing, that you have addressed the following matters.

Make sure your machine is regularly cleaned – lint and broken thread can catch on the mechanisms in the lower section, causing jams or knots in the thread. Use a fine brush, or (better yet) give the under section a quick vacuum (with the foot removed) after every use. This will also keep your sewing machine in better condition in the long run.

Ensure that both the upper and bobbin thread are the same type. It is tempting sometimes to use different colours for decorative or blending effect when sewing, but this can cause problems with knotting or jamming. Try and buy different coloured threads in the same range to reduce this issue.

Check that the tension is correct for both the thread and the fabric type. If you are not sure, use a small sample of the fabric to check if the stitches are the correct size and tension.

Take care to thread your machine correctly. Try not to leave the machine threaded after each job. This will encourage you to rethread the machine before beginning each new sewing session, making sure every aspect in the threading routine is performed correctly. Remember to remove the thread from the lower bobbin.

Check that the thread in the lower bobbin is not caught on the spool case, or any of the machinery. It is surprising how often this happens.

Make sure that the needle is thick enough for the job in hand. It is very irritating when you are trying to get through four or five layers of fabric and – pop! – the needle snaps off. Make sure you know how sturdy your needles need to be before you begin; for instance, whether or not you are going to fold over the fabric a few times before you sew it, so that it is several times the thickness of the original fabric.

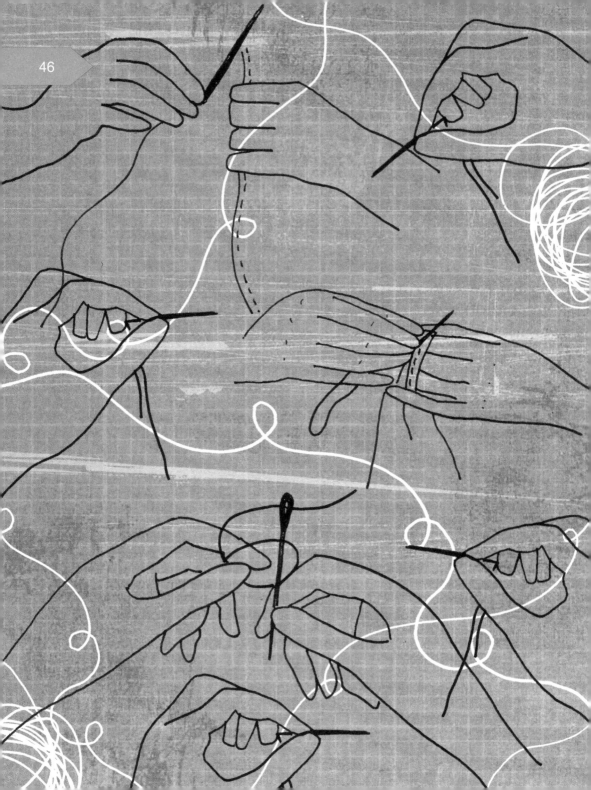

Hand sewing

You will find there are a number of occasions when the only suitable course of action involves hand sewing. Most small tears and holes are much better mended by hand, and several involved projects that will be finished by the sewing machine are best begun with hand-stitched tacks. Similarly, a lot of decorative work is best done by hand, not only for the overall appearance of the work, but also for the calming effect needlecraft has on the nerves. Sometimes, it's better than a day in the spa!

Again (sorry, beginners!), there are hundreds of stitches possible, some remarkably easy and others, well . . . let's just say, I am still, to this day, unable to do a French knot. Here are a number of stitches that should serve you well.

Tacking

This stitch is used as a precursor to permanent stitching (usually on a sewing machine). Make sure you use a needle and thread that is the correct weight for your fabric, or else you may find unsightly holes will remain in your project. Choose a thread of contrasting colour to the fabric, to make the unpicking easier later.

The aim of the tack is purely to keep the fabric together while you test the fit or check seam length. Simply sew in and out in long, even stitches, securing with a double knot.

Diagonal tacking

This is used to hold pleats or multiple layers of fabric together. Instead of a single line of stitches, the thread covers a wider area. Begin at the bottom and sew a long horizontal stitch. Then bring the needle out approx 1cm above the initial entry point. Repeat these long, wide stitches as necessary.

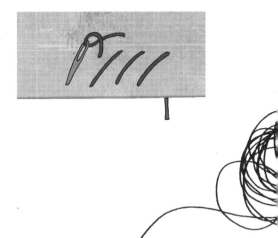

Running stitch

This is the simplest stitch you will come across
and is used predominantly for seams. Using
a similar action to the one used for tacking,
simply secure the thread with a double knot
and sew in and out in a long line. The stitches
may be as long or as short as you require.

Backstitch

This is a brilliant option for seams which is
much stronger than the running stitch. Begin
with a secure knot and sew through the fabric.
Bring the needle back through the fabric
around 4mm to the right of the knot, then sew
back through, or as close to it as you can,
the hole with the knot. Bring the needle back
through the fabric 8mm to the right of the knot,
then go back through the end of the previous
stitch, and so on.

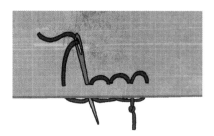

Prickstitch

Using the same principle as backstitch, the
trick here is to work on the right side of the
fabric, making the visible stitches as small as
possible. This is great for sewing in zips or for
seams where the stitches need to be invisible.

Make a knot and sew from the wrong side
through to the right. Bring the needle up through
the fabric, position it 2mm to the left and make a
stitch. Then bring the needle 10mm to the right
of this point and back up through the fabric and
so on. Repeat until finished.

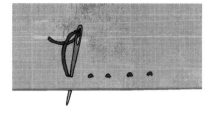

Oversewing

This stitch is used to make raw edges look neater and, used in conjunction with running or backstitch, can help to strengthen seams. Knot your thread and bring your needle through the fabric 3mm from the edge, from the reverse to the front. Pull the thread through and take the needle over the raw edge, bringing it out from the reverse once more, 3mm to the left of the initial hole. Continue taking the thread over the raw edge along the seam. The stitches appear slanted in this method.

Buttonhole stitch

This stitch neatens the raw edges caused by cutting a buttonhole. The premise is very similar to oversewing: you continually bring the needle through from the wrong side of the fabric although, instead of spacing the stitches 2–3mm apart, you space them much closer together. Again, working 2–3mm from the raw edge, knot your thread and bring the needle through from the reverse. Sew over the raw edge and back through, as close to the previous hole as possible.

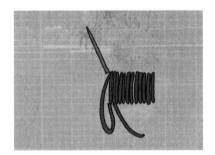

Blanket stitch

This is a decorative stitch for the edges of fabric, most commonly fleeces or woollens, and is frequently achieved using embroidery thread to allow the stitches to be more visible. Knot the thread and, from the reverse, sew through to the front 5–6mm from the raw edge. Pass the needle back over the fabric and through, 3–4mm to the right of the first hole. As you pull the thread out, leave a loop and slip the needle through to catch the thread at the raw edge.

Hemming

The aim of hemming is to fasten the raw edges of a seam to the garment without creating a visible stitch. The best way to do this is to use thread that is the same colour as the garment, a thin needle and a slightly lighter weight than you would use for other sewing. Ensure the hem you are sewing is well ironed and, if possible, use hemming tape to secure the edge. Working with the garment inside out, knot your thread and make a stitch 5mm above the raw edge, through a single layer of fabric (so this doesn't show on the right side), 2mm in length. Then, bring the needle 5mm below the raw edge and catch the needle through a single thread of the fabric (this is the invisible stitch). Bring the needle back 5mm above the raw edge and make another stitch through a single layer of the fabric.

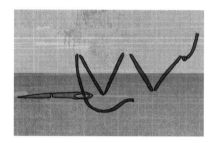

Herringbone stitch

This can also be used for hemming, and is a strong decorative stitch. Knot the thread and sew through a single layer of the hem, bringing the needle back out 3mm to the left. Take the needle diagonally upwards and to the right 10mm, then make another horizontal stitch 3mm in length to the left. Bring the needle back diagonally down and to the right 10mm and repeat the pattern as shown.

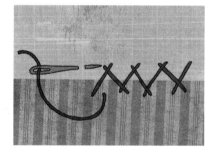

Chain stitch

A very decorative stitch, this is frequently used for securing appliqué. Knot the thread and bring the needle through the fabric from the back to the front. Sew back out, making a stitch 5mm from the original hole. Bring the needle back in, 5mm away again and catch the working thread, making a loop that is held in place by the next stitch. Insert the needle back through the hole it has just emerged from and repeat the process.

Satin stitch

This is frequently used in embroidery to create motifs and is extremely simple to master. It is best produced using 2–3 strands of embroidery silk for filling up larger areas, while using an embroidery ring and some light interfacing to ensure your fabric is taut and does not pull. Your design should be drawn on using a fabric chalk pen, which will fade after 48 hours. Knot your thread and work from the reverse outwards. Decide on the direction of the stitches and begin at the base of the design. Bring the thread from one edge of the design, right across to the other. Bring the needle out next to the initial hole and fill in the design with the thread. If your stitches are a little uneven, or if too much of the base fabric is showing through, try filling in your design with a fabric pen, iron to set, and embroider over the top. This will make your design appear fuller and more complete.

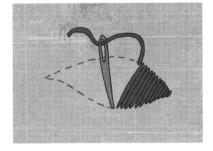

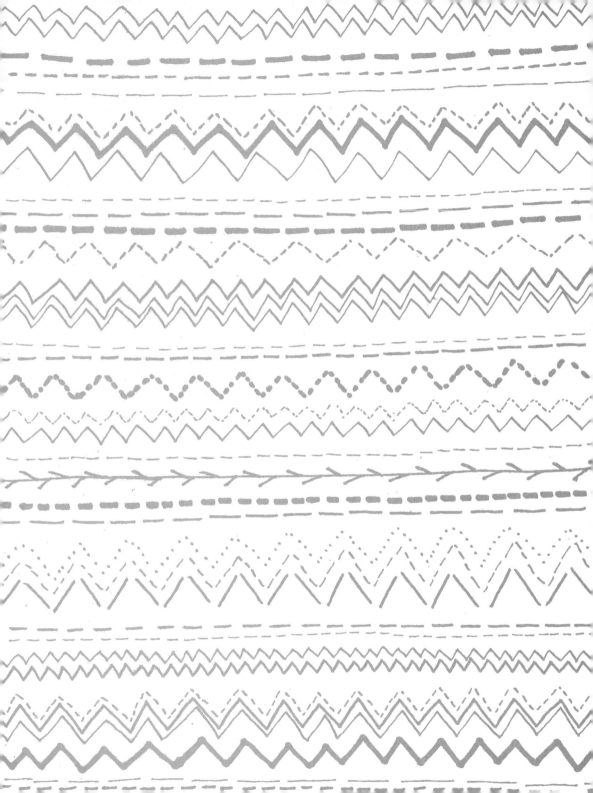

Machine sewing

The number of different stitches your sewing machine will make varies from model to model, though the general consensus is that for 95% of the time you will probably use only 30% of them.
The majority of those 30% are functional stitches: those that allow you to create an item and make it sturdy. The others are usually decorative stitches that can give your finished item a professional look.

Straight stitch

The most basic of stitches, straight stitch provides you with a thin line of neat, even stitches and will make your basic seams adequately. Ensure you have around 10cm of excess thread before beginning, then leave 12–15mm seam allowance from the raw edge of the fabric. Sew along your seam and, as you reach the end, reverse the stitch for 20mm, sewing back over the line. Switch back and sew back along the line to the end. This will secure the stitches, ensuring they do not come undone.

Zigzag stitch

This allows you to neatly finish the raw edge of your fabric, mimicking an overlocker in professionally produced garments. Changing the length of the stitch will alter how close together the zigzag appears, so for overlocking the raw edge of fabric, a longer stitch is better. By shortening the stitch, you can achieve something similar to a buttonhole stitch, which is fantastic for appliqué or patches.

Feather stitch

This is most commonly seen in joining two pieces of suede or leather together and looks similar to herringbone stitch. As leather and similar synthetic fabrics are extremely thick, it is not always suitable to join them in seams as you would usually (i.e. two layers together, sewn on the wrong side). Place the two sections together, side by side, and use feather stitch to join them. The left stitch will catch the left piece and the right... you get the idea.

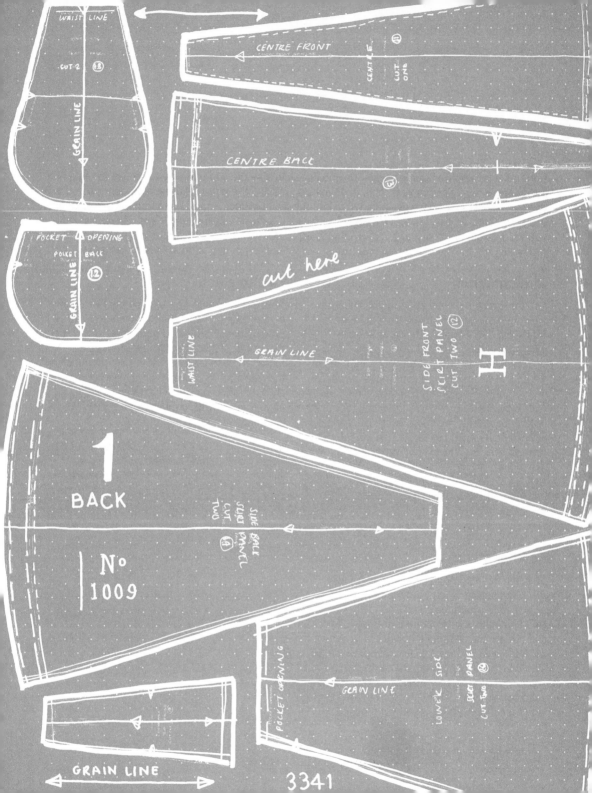

Using patterns

Patterns available from haberdasheries should contain all the information you require to make up the garment to a reasonable standard. Practising making the garment using test fabric will enable you to achieve a more professional finish for your final product, and will also iron out any problems you may come across, without ruining your chosen fabric. If your pattern is a multi-size example, you will need to carefully cut out along the appropriate line. Take care when doing this as a 4mm slip really will mean the difference between a good fit and being unable to button up a shirt.

The patterns will also tell you how much fabric to buy and how to arrange the pattern on the fabric to ensure you have as little wastage as possible.

Checklist

Unless individual instructions say otherwise, keep this checklist to hand and follow the advice given here to ensure success.

1. When you are drawing round patterns, pin your fabric in place to avoid any slips.
2. Always allow for the 10–15mm seam allowance. Any more can get confusing, any less will result in weak seams.
3. Follow the grain and pattern of the fabric. If you are making a pair of trousers, the garment will not feel correct unless the grain of the fabric is running in the same direction. Similarly, try and line up any patterns as much as possible. To do this, fold the fabric lengthways in half, as shown, and cut any duplicate pieces together. This will ensure not only that the pieces are the same, but also that the grain and pattern line up as much as possible. Alternatively, for a more fluid drape (especially for skirts and dresses), rotate your fabric through 45° and cut out the pieces on the bias.

Making seams

Seams are the simplest way of joining two pieces of fabric together. Here are a few basic rules for creating your seam. If you follow them, you will find it easier to produce any type of garment or product.

1. Make sure your pattern is cut out as neatly as possible. Seam allowances are only as accurate as your cutting. If you follow the edge of the material when you are sewing your seam and it is poorly cut out, you will not have a well-fitting or neat product.

2. For complicated garments, always tack pieces of fabric together before machine sewing, to make sure your garment works. It is much easier to unpick tacks than secure machine stitches.

3. Sew over pins, rather than stopping before each one to remove it. This will ensure your stitches are even and straight. Stopping and starting can give loose stitches and your fabric may slip, making the seam uneven.

4. Don't trim excess fabric until you are sure the seam works as it should. If you sew and trim, then realise something is not straight or is too small, you will have nowhere to go as a result.

5. Decide if you need to reinforce the seam with overlocking. This will neaten raw edges as well as providing extra stability.

6. If you are new to sewing, practise using the seam guidelines on the machine, lining up the raw edge of the fabric at the appropriate line, using scraps of fabric.

Plain seams

To make up the seam, place the fabric with right sides together and the raw edges lined up as much as possible. Pin in place, ensuring the pins are at 90° from the seam line. This will allow you to sew over the pins if you do not wish to tack the fabric together. If you do want to tack the seam together, sew using tack (large running stitch) 13mm from the seam edge. This will provide a guide for machine stitching. Remove the pins in this case. Position the fabric under the needle, leaving 15mm seam allowance. Both the fabric edge and the tacking stitches will provide you with a guide for a neat seam. If you cannot see where the needle will go into the fabric, lower the foot and turn the hand wheel on the right side of the machine, gently pushing the needle into the cloth. Reverse the wheel to bring the needle up without making a stitch.

Ensure the settings are correct for your seam, and then gently sew forwards, guiding the fabric for a neat line. When you reach the end, reverse the stitch for 15mm to finish the seam. Remove the tacks and press the seam. If you are happy with the finish, you can trim the raw edge with pinking shears to prevent fraying. Alternatively, using a zigzag stitch on a wide setting, oversew the raw edge. This will provide you with the most professional result.

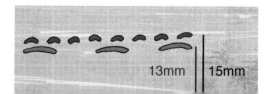

13mm | 15mm

Pivoting

You can continue a seam around a corner without trimming the thread by pivoting around the needle. When you reach a corner, stop 15mm from the end, as shown, with the needle through the fabric. Lift the presser foot and turn the fabric as necessary, pivoting around the needle. When your fabric is lined up correctly, simply lower the foot and continue, ensuring your seam allowance is still in place.

Curved seams

This is very similar to a straight seam, except that once you have sewn the seam, you snip small triangles out of the seam excess, as shown. Once this is done, open out the seam and press flat. This will prevent any misshapen seams.

Ease

Sometimes it is necessary to attach seams where one section of fabric is larger than the other. As such, the raw edges must be eased to fit each other. Take the longer piece and line up the right side of one corner with the right side of the shorter piece. Pin this in place. Line up the other corners and pin, leaving a flat piece of fabric and a curved piece fixed in both corners. Pin at even notches throughout the length of the seam and tack in place, catching

all folds of the fabric. Remove the pins and sew the seam on the machine, as carefully as possible. Remove the tacks and turn inside out to check that the longer side is evenly distributed along the seam.

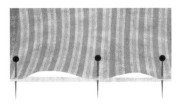

Attaching elastic

Making a seam with elastic is simple. Simply cut a piece of elastic to fit your garment or item and pin at both ends of your fabric. Find the centre and pin again. Pull the elastic to the full length of the fabric and, with the sewing machine on zigzag stitch on a wide setting, sew the seam, keeping the elastic taut at all times.

Decorating fabrics

Fabric pens

These are a quick, easy, creative way of adding personal touches to any project. Work on the fabric before it is made up (unless you are working on bought T-shirts, in which case you should put a layer of foil or cling film between the front and back of the shirt to prevent leaking through to the other side) and place it in a large embroidery ring to keep the fabric taut. See page 98 for a detailed look at using fabric pens.

Appliqué

This is the method of applying shapes of fabric to the surface of a base fabric to produce a design. It can be a successful, attractive and resilient method of decorating fabric, providing striking results with very little effort.

There are a number of ways of producing a motif, with varying degrees of difficulty. Felt appliqué will provide you with quick results as the fabric does not fray easily. Simply cut out the shape, pin it in place on the base fabric and sew on. You can use a variety of stitches by hand, such as running stitch, backstitch or chain stitch. The zigzag function on a sewing machine is particularly helpful, as it not only secures the fabric, but also (if used on a short setting) covers the raw edges of fabric very successfully. Appliqué is very simple, and will provide you with fantastic results if you practise and experiment.

The following stitches can be used in the application of motifs as part of an appliqué.

Running stitch

If your fabric does not fray, or if you require a quick result, sew using running stitch along the outside edge of the fabric. Begin your stitches from the reverse to hide any knots.

Backstitch

This gives a similar effect to running stitch, though there is no gap between the stitches. Again, begin from the reverse to hide knots.

Oversewing

If the stitches are created close together, this will not only hide a raw edge, but also provide an extremely secure finish. The aim is to have one side of the stitch through the motif and the other through the base fabric.

Chain stitch

This is a decorative option for securing fabric that, provided you stick to the edge, will disguise any fraying very nicely.

Creating a patchwork

Yes, those farmhouse quilts or epic hexagonal offerings laboured over by grandmothers throughout history are a great way of using up all those cut-off bits of fabric or holey shirts that will only yield a tiny piece of cloth. However, with modern fabrics and unusual shapes, they don't need to look as old-fashioned as they once did, and they can produce a beautiful piece of work that will last a lifetime.

The first step to a successful patchwork is creating a template. The patchwork itself is made up of small sections so, if your pieces are not accurately cut, you won't achieve a neat product. Make your shape using a piece of stiff card; something that won't fall to pieces once you've drawn round it ten times. Cereal packets will do, thick cardboard is great, ice cream tubs are best as the plastic is thin enough to be cut with scissors and will keep for ever. You can buy templates from craft stores for the traditional shapes, which are useful for getting angles correct, but you can easily make them yourself.

It is best to sketch out the design of your patchwork before you begin. Amass together the fabric you have at your disposal and use some graph paper to draft your design based on the resources you have.

When you are piecing together your patchwork, be patient, work slowly and be as accurate as possible. Ensure your seam allowances are consistent and do not guess. It can be extremely difficult to line up the most basic of shapes if they are not placed properly. You can mark off the seam allowance with a fabric pen if necessary.

Creating a basic patchwork

Step one
Ensure all the fabric you are using is clean and well pressed. It is impossible to neatly cut out a shape from creased fabric. Lay out the fabric face down with the grains running in the same direction. If you are cutting through a few layers of fabric, make sure they are stacked with the grain running vertically throughout.

Step two
Place your template on the fabric, ensuring the design is the right way up. Draw round the template and cut it out carefully. Make sure you have left a seam allowance of 10mm.

Step three
Pin two patches with right sides together, ensuring the pins run at 90° to the direction of the seam. Ensure the patch is completely aligned.

Step four
Sew along the seam carefully using backstitch or a straight stitch on your machine. Repeat this process with another two patches.

Step five
To join these two sections together, open them out and press flat. Then, treat them as smaller sections, pinning together and sewing. When finished, press again.

It is best to sew sections in a line, then join two lines together, and so on. The patchwork can be used in a number of projects; simply treat the newly created design as a piece of fabric to be used in the normal way.

Using scraps of fabric

If you have lots of small scraps of fabric that are similar in weight, it is possible to join them together in a 'crazy' patchwork. This can work very well if you think about the colours before starting. Try keeping to two or three complementary colours, or interspersing patterns with a plain linen or cotton to stop your patchwork looking like an explosion in a fabric shop.

With crazy patching you won't need to be quite so precious about seams or hemming. Simply place two pieces of fabric together, right sides facing, pin them together and sew one edge. You will find it much easier and quicker if you use a machine straight stitch to do this. Keep joining sections, trying to use two different shades next to each other as frequently as possible. If you don't have a piece to fit perfectly, simply cut one to shape. Eventually you'll have a large piece of fabric that will make a brilliant cushion or bag.

A good idea when storing offcuts is to cut them into right-angled triangles. This will mean that any future crazy patching projects you have will be easier to fit together. Store the pieces in plastic wallets or box files, either in like colours or sizes. This will make life much easier in the long run.

2

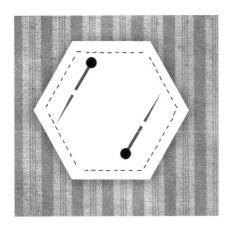

3

4

5

Dealing with stains

There are many garments in my wardrobe that have remained resolutely on the hanger purely owing to the fact that I am somewhat clumsy. The most common culprits are red wine and chocolate, but let's gloss over that and face the fact that stains on clothes are one of the most common reasons for throwing away our togs.

Many stains can be removed with a little effort, but without a single stitch, so try using the wealth of brightly packaged stain removers out there before resorting to the needle. If the stain won't budge, here are a few suggestions to try.

Patch it

Drips or spills over shirts or T-shirts can be easily covered with a small embroidered patch, which you can purchase from haberdashers or online. Iron-on patches are also available, and are a good quick fix, though you are recommended to sew them on afterwards as a precaution. Alternatively, you can make your own decorative patch easily (see the patching section). It's best to consider the overall look of the garment before patching, as a single small design may look strange if positioned badly. If your stain is in a place where a single patch may look silly, consider using a few patches or motifs to make the design look more interesting.

Colour it with a fabric pen

Bleach spots on dark T-shirts can be covered using a fabric pen. These are available in hundreds of colours and can be blended to match directly the colour of the garment. Once you've coloured the stain in, iron the garment on a warm setting to set the colour and ensure it's washable.

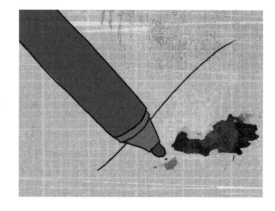

Dye it

Does the stain cover more than 5% of the fabric? If so, consider dyeing the garment.   This is particularly successful for bleach spots on dark fabrics, or dark spots on lighter fabrics, if you don't mind turning your garment dark all over. There are a number of home dyeing products that give extremely good results, and you can make the operation a more economical option by treating a few garments together. However, dyeing can produce unexpected and uneven results, with some fabrics not taking the chemicals well at all. Make sure you follow the instructions as closely as possible to avoid potential disasters.

Cover it with embroidery

Stains can also be covered using plain embroidery. Choose some embroidery thread that is the closest match you can find to the garment and cover the area entirely with small satin stitches. Alternatively, let your creativity run riot and embellish your garment with patterns, beads and sequins. You may find a plain old T-shirt turning into your favourite 'going out' top. If you are going to embroider a design, use some light interfacing behind to ensure it does not pull, and place both layers of fabric into an embroidery ring.

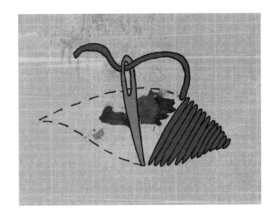

Cover it with a pocket

A strategically placed pocket can give adequate cover for the stain, as well as providing you with a useful place to store your change. Pockets can be made easily from scrap fabric by cutting out the desired shape, including a 15mm seam allowance along the top and 5mm all round the remainder. Fold the top seam down and iron flat. Repeat along the other seams. Pin the pocket into place and sew along the sides and bottom edge.

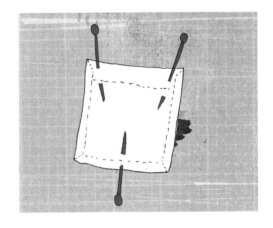

Mending your garments

Small seam tears

These are the simplest of mends and can be done quickly and efficiently by hand. Simply turn the garment inside out and pin the hole together. Choose the strongest thread of a suitable grade for your fabric and knot well. Using a short backstitch, sew along the existing seam line, keeping the stitches even and taut. Once you have reached the edge, reinforce the seam by oversewing back along the seam line.
Secure with a double knot.

Always try to catch tears in fabrics when they are small, to ensure your garment has the longest possible life. Similarly, it's best to catch the tear as soon as it is done, to ensure the fibres of the fabric tear or fray as little as possible, so don't wash the garment before mending.

Tears in fabric

Tears within the fabric are a little more difficult to deal with. Again, the patching route is an easy, pain-free solution for many problem holes, though this can be rather too conspicuous for some garments.

Using fabric glues

There are a number of products that allow you to mend small tears using adhesives, removing the need for sewing. These glues are usually permanent and waterproof, and are excellent for heavyweight fabrics, although they can show through delicate types.

L-shaped tears

These can be mended using iron-on mending tape. Simply close the tear, as close as possible, and place the mending tape over the tear on the reverse side of the fabric. Once the tape is bonded to the fabric, you may wish to blend the tear by using a series of small stitches. Choose the correct thread for your fabric and as close a colour match as possible. Knot the end and, beginning from the reverse to the right side of the fabric, use very small, even stitches to oversew the join of the tear. Try and make sure the stitches follow the grain of the fabric, so that the tear is as invisible as possible.

Holes

Though the need for the mothball has lessened with the rise of synthetic fabrics, holes are still an issue, especially in knitted or woven clothes. There are two options for holes: patching or darning. The choice you take in mending your hole depends directly on how visible you want the repair to be. Patching usually leaves a tell-tale pull or stitch, whereas darning, if done correctly, can blend invisibly into the fabric.

Patching from the reverse

Small holes in trousers can be patched by taking a little of the same fabric from the hem. Cut a patch large enough to cover the hole and place the garment in an embroidery ring. Place the patch behind the hole and pin. Using thread of a similar weight to the fabric, sew all around the hole using tiny stitches, blending the two layers of fabric together. This type of mend should not be used for conspicuous areas, as this will be noticeable.

Visible patching

You may wish to make the patch a decorative feature by using a contrasting fabric. This works particularly well with children's clothes (especially boys' trousers), which are more prone to wear and tear (especially if they enjoy skidding on their knees) and will frequently have quite large holes in them. Cut a piece of fabric to fully cover the hole and pin it behind. Tack the patch in place. Using embroidery thread, sew by hand all around the patch, either with matching thread or (if you really want it to stand out) a complementary colour.

Patching from the right side

As we have already mentioned, it is possible to buy ready-made patches that simply require sewing or ironing in place. T-shirts can benefit from a motif patch, which will neatly cover stains or holes. It is sometimes beneficial to place the T-shirt in an embroidery ring for ease of sewing and also to ensure the T-shirt does not ruche or pull as a heavy patch is placed on top of it.

Darning

Holes in knitted or woven fabrics are best fixed by darning them closed. The darn mimics the warp and weft of the thread, in effect rebuilding the fabric and closing the hole. It is best, if possible, to use threads taken from the fabric itself, either from within the hem or at a seam. If this is not possible, choose a thread that is most similar to that which makes up the fabric, both in colour and texture.

You will find a darning mushroom extremely useful, especially in repairing socks, as this spreads the fabric and holds it in place while you work. If you do not have one, try using a piece of cardboard or, if even this is unavailable, your free hand inside the garment will work just as well. Use a darning needle, which is blunt and long, and shouldn't (unless you're really trying) hurt if you accidentally catch yourself.

1. Place the mushroom or your hand behind the hole and sew a line of stitches 4–5mm from the bottom of the hole, beginning 4mm to the right of the hole and finishing 4mm to the left.

2. Repeat this line of stitches 1mm closer to the hole, and again until you reach the hole itself.

3. Begin another row of stitches. When you reach the hole, take your thread across the hole and continue the stitches on the other side. Repeat this again, each time creeping 1mm up the hole to recreate the weft of the thread. Continue past the hole with a line of short stitches the width of the hole.

4. Turn the fabric through 90° and repeat the process, creating the warp threads. As you come to fill the hole, weave your needle in and out of the previously made weft. Ensure you stitch at least 4mm from the edge of the hole to strengthen your darning.

5. When you have finished, take the thread to the wrong side and make a few small stitches to secure the thread. Knot well.

If the hole to be darned is very large, use a piece of lightweight woven fabric behind the hole to sew into and secure your stitches, strengthening the mend.

1&2

3

4

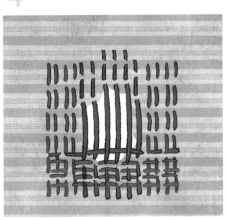

5

Zips

Repairing a zip

There is nothing worse than pulling on your favourite jeans, only to find the fly has broken. Zips are notoriously difficult to repair and, when they have broken once, they are likely to break again. The best thing to do is replace the zip or, if that's too much like hard work, turn the jeans into a tote bag. Here is a temporary repair for a zip whose puller has come off the rails.

1. Pull the zip as wide open as possible. On the side where the runner has come away, cut in between the zip teeth 10mm from the base.

2. Feed the lower part of the zip (the portion that is above the cut) into the zip puller and close it, ensuring the teeth are aligned correctly.

3. Thread a needle with strong thread and sew the zip together 2mm above the cut. Make several stitches, sewing over the same spot to act as a barrier for the zip puller. For a more permanent option, cover the sewing with superglue, being careful not to spill it anywhere on the garment.

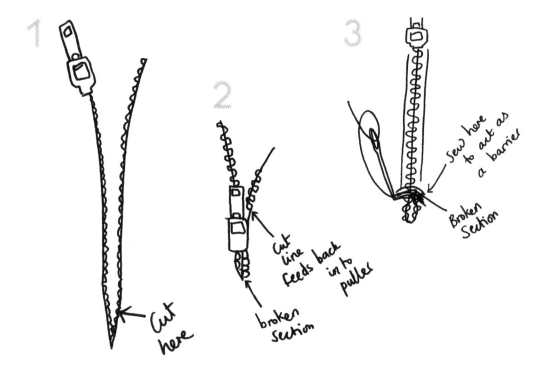

Inserting a zip

For me this was always a troublesome exercise, mainly due to the fact (as already established) that I am impatient. However, if you follow these instructions and have patience, it shouldn't be too arduous.

Zips work best when inserted at a seam, as there is a large amount of fabric to attach the fixing to; however, it is possible to sew them directly into the fabric. There are three basic types of sewn-in zip, described below.

Exposed zip

This type uses a section of fabric that is not a seam. The teeth of the zip are fully exposed for ease of opening.

Concealed zip

Utilising a seam to cover the zip, especially in dresses, allows the look of the fabric to remain uncompromised by the fixing.

Open-ended zip

As used in jackets, this allows you to open the garment completely. The teeth of the zip are usually exposed for ease of opening, though the zip can be closed off with a flap of fabric.

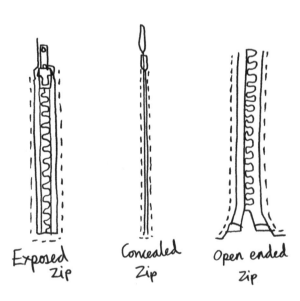

Exposed Zip   Concealed Zip   Open ended Zip

Using a zipper foot

A wonderful invention to make the sewing machine user's life so much easier, this has only one prong rather than two, allowing the side that abuts against the zip to be unimpeded. Ensure the foot is set to the left of the needle, to allow you to see the guides on the needle plate. You can now use this foot as usual.

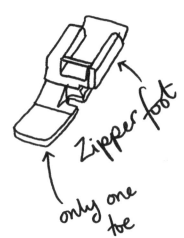

Zipper foot

only one toe

Shortening a zip

It is almost impossible to find zips that will fit your own projects properly, as it is rare for you to use standard measurements. As such, you can buy a polyester zip that is an inch or two longer than necessary. Simply identify and mark where you would wish your zip to end and, using strands of a thick embroidery thread, sew over the teeth of the closed zip to secure it in place. This should stop the zip slider from going beyond your chosen point.

Once the zip is secure, you can simply trim off the excess (leaving 15mm allowance) with strong shears. Avoid using metal zips for this job.

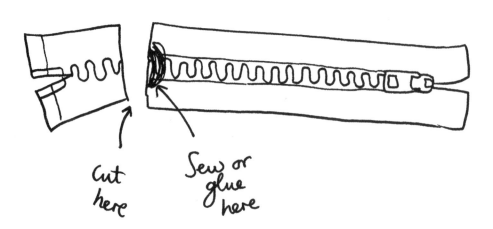

Cut here

Sew or glue here

Creating a lapped zip

This is used for inserting a zip at a seam, for example in skirts or trousers.

1. Leave a gap in the end of the seam where the zip will be placed. Lay the garment right side down and press the seam open, with a flap of fabric to the left and right, continuing beyond the edge of the seam and to the edge of the material.

2. Pin the zip tape in place behind the right-hand edge of the gap. Ensure the teeth lie directly underneath the edge of the opening.

3. Tack the zip in place, remove the pins and stitch along the seam, ensuring the teeth of the zip are on the right of the zipper foot. When you reach the zip slider, stop sewing, carefully slide the zip closed (and past the foot), then continue to the end. Remove the tacking.

4. Repeat the process with the left side, ensuring that when the opening is laid flat, the zip is not visible. Not only will this create a neater look, but also, as the fabric is not pulled outwards, your garment won't lose its shape. Sew carefully from the top of the zip to the bottom, then pivot using the needle and sew along the base to stop the zip slider from coming away from the zip.

It is possible to create a lapped zip and continue the seam past the zip (this is used mainly for pockets in bags). To do this, use the same process as above, but instead of having an open end, simply leave a gap in the seam large enough for the zip to be sewn in.

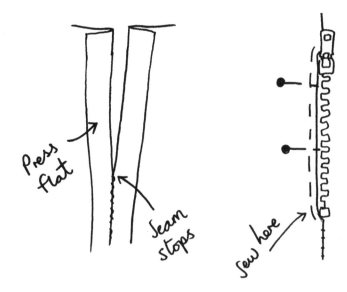

Buttons and buttonholes

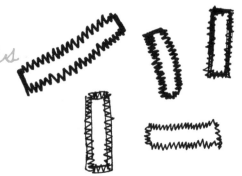

Buttons are a very common method of closing fabric and, thanks to the miracles of modern sewing machines, it's now much easier to sew them on and to make buttonholes. For a professional finish you should use the machine and a seam ripper, though it is possible to do these jobs by hand.

Sewing on buttons and making buttonholes by hand

Identify and mark out where you wish to place your button. Thread your needle with strong thread and knot well at the base. Sew a series of small stitches in a cross where you wish to place your button. Then, for buttons with four holes, thread the button onto your needle and sew diagonally to the next hole. Repeat this three to four times and then move on to the other two holes. Return to the original hole and sew into the hole to the left, repeating three to four times. Repeat this for the other two holes. When you are happy that the button is secure, come out to the back of the fabric, sew over the stitches (catching the sewing and not returning to the right side of the cloth) a few times, knot twice and trim the excess thread.

To make the corresponding buttonhole, measure the button and mark out the position where you wish the hole to be placed. Using a seam ripper, cut the hole into the fabric, erring on the side of caution in relation to its size: it's best to have a snug fit, as the buttonhole will stretch with use, and a hole that is too big is of no use to anyone. Test the hole on your button. If the button goes through too easily, you can sew the hole closed slightly to make it work. It should take a little effort to push the button through, but not resemble an Olympic sport. If you're happy with the hole, you can set about covering it (remember, this will shave a few millimetres off the diameter of the hole, so bear this in mind when you are testing).

1. Start approximately 3mm from the top of the hole and, using a strong thread, sew a large buttonhole stitch at the head of the hole, covering the length of two shorter stitches.

2. Continue sewing down to reach the hole, with stitches not more than 0.8mm apart, and then oversew the left side of the hole, all the way to the base. You are, in effect, covering up the raw edge of the fabric.

3. When you reach the base, repeat the larger stitches to finish the look and travel up the right-hand side, covering the remaining raw edge of the hole. When you meet the top, sew a couple more of the longer stitches, knot and trim the thread. This should provide you with a neat, professional finish.

Sewing on buttons and making buttonholes using a machine

It is best to refer to the instructions of your particular model of sewing machine for sewing on buttons and making buttonholes, as the instructions can vary from machine to machine. Needless to say, it is possible to sew on buttons using a machine, but I have always found that hand-sewn buttons are more secure.

As for buttonholes, the finish you get from your machine is infinitely better, not to mention less time-consuming. Again, refer to your manual, but the basic premise is the same for all machines. It will probably involve turning the stitch dial to complete the different stages.

Pleats

It might not seem an essential technique for a beginner to learn, but the ability to pleat fabric is extremely useful as a decorating tool. Pleating allows you to quickly and efficiently change the texture of fabric, making a plain old piece of cotton interesting, tactile and delicate. A well-pleated piece of fabric instantly appears more expensive and elegant, whether you are using it for skirts, bags or cushions. So let's get on with it, shall we?

Unpatterned fabric is best for pleating, though this is by no means a rule you have to cling to. Indeed, horizontal pleats on a vertical stripe will look lovely if done well, although the lines will give away any poor or skewed folds.

Pleats are formed using a template, consisting of three lines. The first, the internal fold line, is the point at which the fabric is folded back on itself. The second, the placement line, is the point at which the pleat is folded to. The third, the pleat edge, is the point at which the fabric doubles back on itself. The distance between the folds and the direction in which the fabric is folded determines what type of pleat is created. Remember, when cutting fabric that is to be pleated, you will need at least three times the length of fabric that you would ordinarily use. As a result, pleated fabrics are much warmer and stronger, as they are made up of several layers.

There are two basic types of pleat, both equally easy to produce with a little practice and effort.

Knife pleat pattern

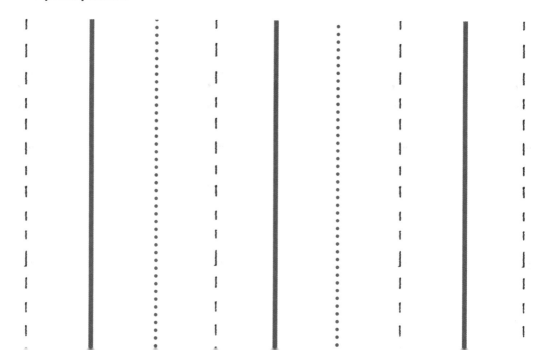

Knife pleats

The recognisable fold seen on many a school uniform, knife pleats are formed using a single fold and placement line. When viewed from the hem, they resemble a zigzag, and are usually made in a single direction. They can be produced in two directions, as they are worked from the centre in one direction and mirrored on the other side.

To create a knife pleat

First draw your pattern. Take a sheet of paper, turn it to landscape position and draw a line in a coloured pen on the left-hand side of your sheet. This will be your first placement line. Decide on the depth of your pleat and measure that distance to the right from the first line. Draw your second line in a different colour. This will be your first internal fold line. Measure the same amount again to the right of the second line and draw a third line in another colour. This will be your pleat edge. Repeat this pattern of colours along the paper.

Place the template on the right side of your fabric and mark out the lines. If you have time, use different coloured threads and tack along the lines (you can rip the template away after completing). Ensure the marks are clear if you do not choose to tack.

Starting at the left, fold the fabric back on itself along the first internal fold line.
Fold the fabric back in the opposite direction as it reaches the placement line. Your pleat edge should line up with the pleat edge line. Pin this in place securely, going through all layers of fabric.

Form the next pleat by folding the fabric back on itself at the next internal fold line. Repeat the process of lining up with placement lines and folding back along pleat edge lines. Ensure you pin each pleat in place as you go, taking care to go through all layers of fabric.

Tack through each pleat, moving at 90° to the direction of the folds. Make sure you sew through all layers of the fabric to keep the pleat in place.

With a dry iron, press the pleats well. For delicate fabrics you may need to use a pressing cloth. Your pleats are now in place. Remove the tacking when you have sewn the fabric to a support, such as a waistband or seam.

Box pleats

These are built up from two knife pleats folded in opposite directions so that they are facing each other, creating a box with two sides and a base. Equal box pleats have folds that lie next to each other.

To create a box pleat

You will need to create a slightly different pattern for box pleats. Starting from the left-hand side of your paper, and using your coloured pens as described for knife pleats, you will need to draw a pleat edge line, then an internal fold line, then a placement line, followed by another internal fold line and a pleat edge line. This pattern should be repeated along the length of the paper.

Mark your pleats, taking into account the new pattern. Starting from the left, ignore the first pleat edge line and fold the fabric in to the right. At the placement line, fold the first pleat edge line back on itself. Pin this in place.

Move on to the next internal fold line and fold the fabric back towards the left. Fold the pleat edge to meet the opposite pleat at the previous placement line. Pin this in place.

Repeat the pattern, creating individual box pleats, pinning as you go. Repeat the process of tacking to secure the pleats just as described for knife pleats.

A good tip for testing your template is simply to fold the paper to mimic the way your pleats would work on your fabric. Remember, your pleats do not need to be fully even all the way through; the distance between the next pleat can be as short or as long as you wish, though a rule of thumb (so as not to use too much fabric) is, try not to make the distances less than the size of the fold itself.

Box pleat pattern

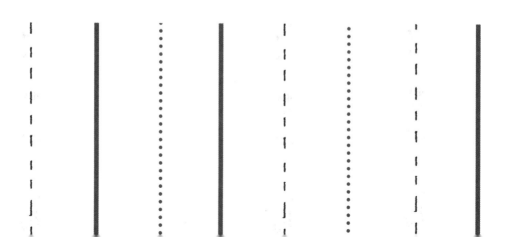

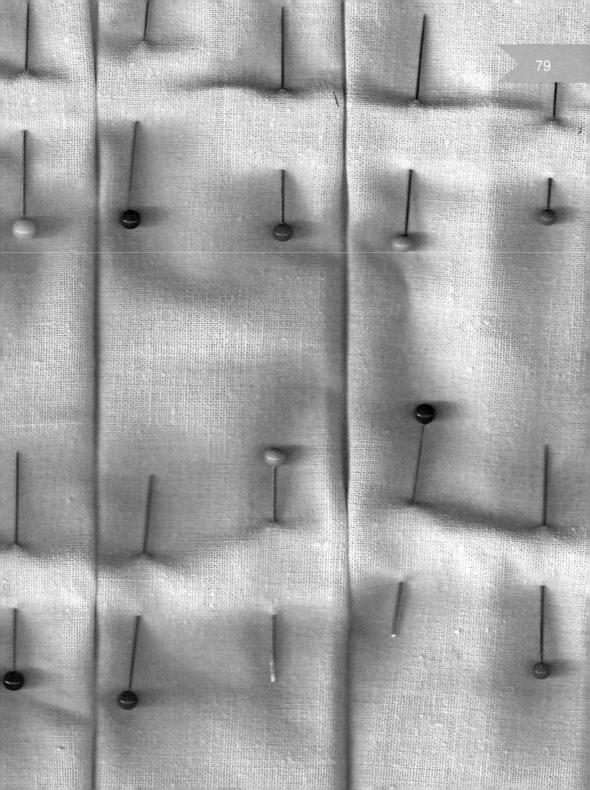

Notes and Ideas

For all the projects in this book, you will need at the very minimum:

cotton or polyester thread;
embroidery threads;
needles;
scissors;
seam ripper;
pins;
tailor's chalk (or similar for marking patterns).

These items will make the projects much easier, quicker and neater:

sewing machine;
denim needles;
embroidery ring;
fabric pens;
a range of coloured thread;
ribbon;
embroidery scissors.

(* tea and biscuit
optional)

Making scarves

I am somewhat addicted to scarves, partly because I am constantly cold and partly because of their ability to instantly enliven my usual black top/trousers combination. They are also extremely easy to make from old clothes, and are a fantastic beginner's item as they are, in essence, just rectangles of fabric.

OLD BLOUSE SCARF

Delicate blouses or skirts in chiffon or silk are extremely difficult to repair, as mends are too visible and heavy patches ruin the drape. They are, however, terribly easy to turn into pretty headscarves or neckerchiefs. They also make brilliant presents for ladies who are difficult to buy for.

You will need

1 sheer fabric blouse or sheer fabric, at least 700mm square

To make

1. Lay the clean and pressed (if possible) garment open on a flat surface.

2. Identify the largest seam-free area and mark out a square shape.

3. Cut the shape out carefully, ensuring the fabric is taut and as wrinkle free as possible. A neater raw edge will result in a neater seam.

4. Fold over the edge of the fabric 5mm all round and press to ensure a neat finish.

5. Repeat this to disguise the raw edge of the fabric and pin down as shown.

6. Using a sewing machine, straight stitch the seam closed all round. Try using a contrasting colour for a decorative finish.

STEPS
4 & 5

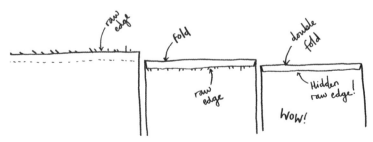

As modelled by Bertie

Why not try using any leftover sections of fabric to make this bag scarf to liven up a drab handbag.

1. Using the same method as above, cut a section that is shaped as shown in the illustration; 400 x 100mm works best, but you can experiment with different sizes.
2. Simply tie this round the handle of your bag for a cheerful decoration. Try threading a large bead on it before tying the knot, to make it even more attractive.

Alternatively, cut leftovers into neat rectangles and store them for future use, or why not try making the wreath on page 136?

PATCHWORK SCARF

Tom Baker's incarnation of Doctor Who may have sported a knitted scarf, but there is nothing to stop you creating a stylish, recycled fabric version of it. It may not enable you to conquer time and space, but it will definitely keep you warm. This works best when all the patches are from fabrics of a similar weight and thickness, so try and keep this in mind when choosing material. Jersey and T-shirt fabric work particularly well.

You will need

At least 2000mm in length of different fabrics

To make

1. Gather as many different fabrics as you can but, to prevent the scarf from looking too eccentric,* try to limit yourself to no more than five different colours/patterns and include a couple of neutral tones, such as beige, grey or brown.

2. Decide on the width of your scarf. I would recommend 200–250mm, but it is your project.

3. Cut rectangular pieces from your fabric that are twice your chosen width, but different lengths. Here is a guide for your pattern, though this can be adapted as you wish.

4. Pin two pieces of contrasting fabric together and sew using straight stitch, leaving a seam allowance of no more than 8mm.

5. Continue to add fabric to your scarf to grow the length as shown below. Try to keep the fabrics that touch as different as possible.

6. Lay the scarf flat on an ironing board and press the seams. This will give a neater finish.

7. Fold the scarf in half lengthways, with the seams out, as shown. Pin along the length and press again.

8. Sew along the length of the scarf to create a tube. Turn this inside out and press flat.

9. Fold in the top and bottom seams and pin closed. Using straight stitch, finish the scarf by sewing the pinned seams together.

*Eccentricity is in the eye of the beholder. If you like lots of colours/ patterns together, then go for it!

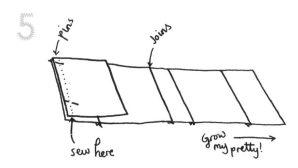

pins

Joins

sew here

Grow my pretty!

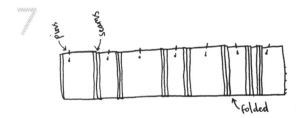

pins

seams

folded

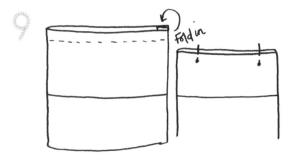

Fold in

Cut lengths of 120–140mm to make a fringe. Simply place between the top and bottom seams before pinning, and then sew closed.

T-SHIRT COWL SCARF

I love this; not only is it ridiculously easy to make, but it keeps you delightfully warm if you line it with a fleece fabric. I've even made one from a Led Zeppelin T-shirt to ensure my rock credentials remain intact while keeping warm at gigs. This works well with stained T-shirts, as you can simply turn the shirt inside out.

You will need

A T-shirt
Lining material (if you wish) – 1200 x 1000mm

To make

1. Ensure your T-shirt is clean and pressed.

2. Cut off the sleeves and neckline. This will leave you with a large, rectangular tube of fabric. If you would like to line your cowl, follow the instructions in step 3. If not, go straight to step 4.

3. Using a fleece or knitted fabric for warmth (this could be an old jumper or blanket), cut a piece the same size as your cowl to act as the lining. When measuring against your T-shirt, don't forget to fold over the warm fabric to ensure you cut enough. If necessary, sew the fleece along the side seam, as shown, to create another tube. Place the T-shirt tube inside the lining tube, inside out, so that the design will be visible when your cowl is turned the right way.

4. With the tubes both inside out, fold over the top seam 10mm, press and pin. If you have lined your cowl, ensure you catch the raw edge of your lining fabric underneath the folded T-shirt as shown.

5. Carefully sew along the seam, ensuring you are not catching the other edge as you go.

6. Repeat steps 4 and 5 for the other seam. Your cowl is now complete.

Why not try popping a vintage brooch on your cowl to decorate it. Or perhaps sew on a contrasting bow for a bit of added glamour?

2   Cut here   3   fleece inside   4   folded edge (cover the inside fleece)

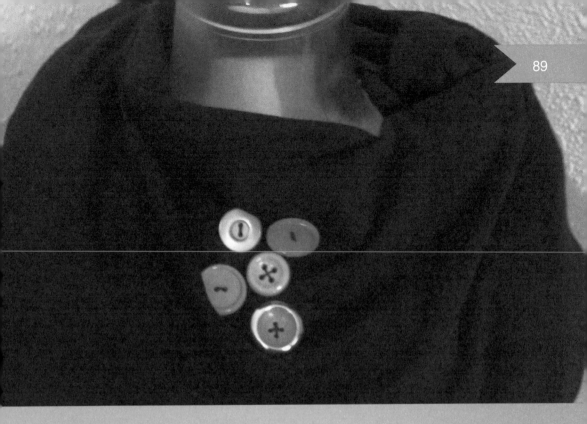

MAKE IT LACY

You can make a more open version of this by slicing open the T-shirt tube and joining the gap using lace, net or another decorative fabric. Hem the T-shirt fabric and pin the lace underneath. You can either close the tube by joining the other side of the tube to the lace, or simply leave it open. Try twinning navy blue or grey fabric with beige or flesh-toned net for a chic style.

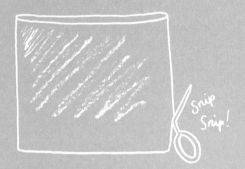

Snip Snip!

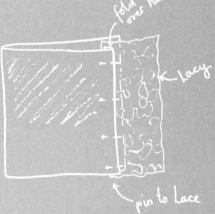

fold over hem

Lacy

pin to Lace

RUCHED JERSEY SCARF

Not only is this remarkably warm, but also it looks great with a simple coat. An offcut piece of jersey can be picked up for less than £3 in most haberdasheries, or can be pilfered from an old dress, skirt or cardigan. The ruching works best with a single piece of fabic, as seams or joins will interrupt the design.

You will need

2000mm jersey fabric
Embroidery silk

To make

1. Cut a section of fabric roughly 2000 x 350mm. As neatly cut jersey doesn't fray, you may not need to hem this. However, if you prefer to do so, simply fold over the sides and sew.

2. Thread all six strands of a length of embroidery silk into a thick, sharp needle and knot the end. Lay the fabric out flat on a table and mark two points at one end, splitting the fabric into three sections as shown.

3. Using simple tacking stitch, sew a straight line of stitches, roughly 15mm long, along the length of the fabric, leaving a tail of 150mm. When you reach the end, knot the thread to secure. Repeat this along the other line as shown.

4. To ruche the scarf, push the fabric against the thread to gather. Pull and push the fabric to neaten the gathered fabric as needed. Repeat along the other line.

5. When you are happy with your ruching, rethread the needle with the embroidery silk and sew over the edge of the fabric five or six times to secure the thread. Knot well and trim. Repeat with the other edge.

STEPS

2&3

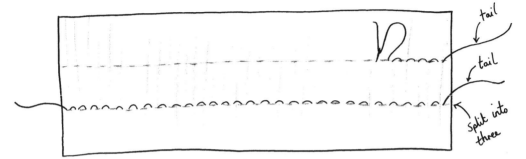

tail

tail

Split into three

4

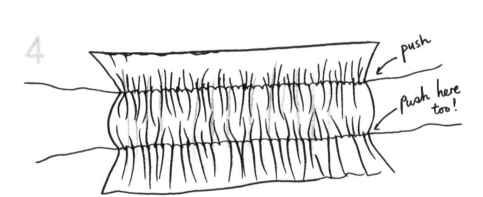

push

Push here too!

Why not try making an alternative version of this by slicing small holes into the fabric at intervals of 30mm as shown. Then, using ribbon of your choice, weave in and out of the holes in a long line. Pull the fabric as before and sew over the ribbon to secure it at each end.

5

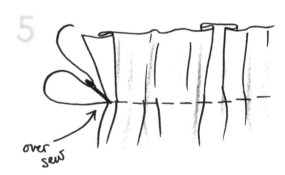

over sew

Making bags

Bags really can be an easy option to make, especially if you are creative with items such as handles. It is a good idea to invest in an eyelet tool, which will allow you to create strong fixings for a number of projects. Don't be afraid to buy D rings as they provide strength, versatility and also an extremely professional finish.

BASIC TOTE

Now that the plastic carrier bag is anathema to those of us who care about the environment (and, in certain shops, about our purses too), you can't have too many tote bags. Totes have become as popular as T-shirts as a way of expressing individualism and, because they are so easy to create, you can make them as simple or as sophisticated as your tastes and talents allow.

You will need

1500mm fabric

To make

1. Your bag can be as large or as small as you like, though two pieces of fabric 420 x 570mm will give you a good-sized tote.

2. Place the two pieces of fabric with the right sides together and pin. Sew using straight stitch along the two sides and bottom, as shown, leaving a 10mm seam allowance.

3. Using the zigzag function on your sewing machine, on a wide setting, sew along the raw edges of the fabric next to the seam. This will neaten the seam inside and also provide added strength to your bag.

4. Fold over the top edge 10mm and press. If necessary, repeat this to disguise the raw edge.

5. Pin and sew the top hem using straight stitch, ensuring that the lower bobbin thread on your machine blends with the fabric colour (as this will be visible). Take care to sew one layer of fabric at a time, as I have frequently sewn my bags closed by accident! You will be able to sew the entire seam in one long loop.

6. Turn the bag the right way out and press all the seams to ensure the shape of the bag is as neat as possible.

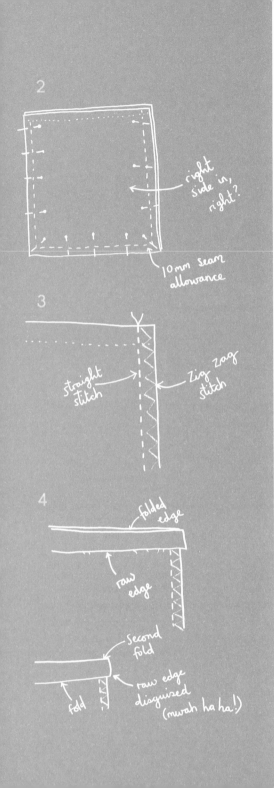

2

right side in, right?

10 mm seam allowance

3

straight stitch

Zig Zag stitch

4

folded edge

raw edge

Second fold

fold

raw edge disguised (mwah ha ha!)

This bag was made using fabric designed by textile artist Georgia Coote. You can see more of her work by visiting her website: www.georgiacoote.co.uk/

The general rule for making a tote bag is always to consider what you will use it for. If you intend to carry around the equivalent of the complete works of Shakespeare, it is best to make sure the fabric you use is strong enough to cope with such weight. So opt for strong, woven fabrics such as thick cotton, linen, denim, tweed or calico.

5

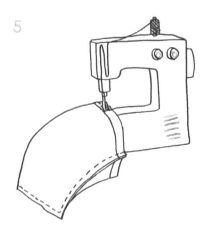

Making handles

There are a number of options for the handles of your tote bag.

TRADITIONAL MATCHING HANDLES

1. Cut two lengths of fabric suitable for your use, and fold in half, pressing the side seam for a clean edge.

2. Lay the fabric flat on a table, outer side down and fold in half.

3. Fold the raw edges in towards the centre and close them in as shown.

4. Press again to neaten the seams and pin.

5. Sew along the open edge. Repeat the process for the other handle.

6. Place the handle inside the bag, with each end 70mm from the edge of the bag. Pin in place and repeat on the other side with the remaining handle. Ensure your handles are equal in length.

7. For a strong join, machine sew along the bottom edge of all four joins, then again 30mm from this. For a professional finish, sew a rectangle with a cross inside as shown.

ROPE HANDLES

1. Cut two lengths of rope, as long as you require, plus an extra 20mm for knotting the ends.

2. Using an eyelet tool, make two holes in one side of your bag, each one 30mm from the top hem and 70mm from one side. Repeat on the other side of the bag.

3. Thread one end of one handle from the outside in and create a large knot on the inside of the bag to prevent the handle from slipping through. Thread the other end through the second hole and make another knot. Repeat with the second handle on the other side.

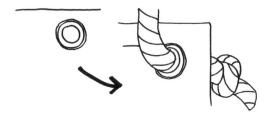

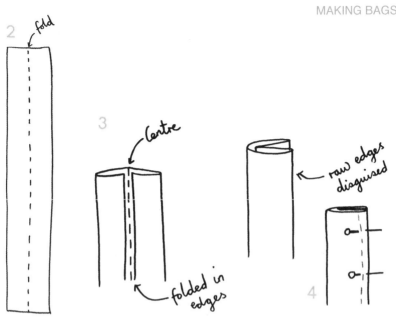

2 fold

3 centre

raw edges disguised

folded in edges

4

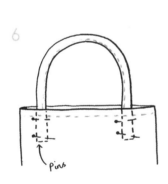

6

pins

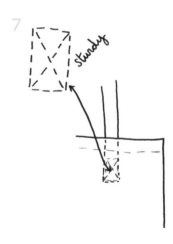

7 sturdy

DECORATIVE TIE HANDLES

Men's ties are not only decorative but also extremely strong. They can enliven a plain bag and provide a stylish alternative to beige handles. This is a great way to use unwanted or damaged ties. It's best to use striped ties, as any sewing can be disguised within the design.

1. Choose a tie for your bag. Pin the thicker end of the tie on the front of the bag. Pin the thinner end inside the bag, on the opposite side. Try and keep both ends 70mm from the side seams.

2. Using a strong thread matching your tie, join thick end of the tie to the bag by sewing a series of lines. If your tie has a stripe, follow the diagonal line with your stitches. If not, keep the stitches horizontal.

3. Fix the thin end to the inside of your bag in the same way.

See page 94 for more ideas for handles

Business bag

I say!

Gentleman's tie

Decorating a tote bag

There are so many ways you can make your tote your own that it is impossible to show them all here. It is easier to decorate the tote before you sew it together, so identify which side you want to be the 'front' and work on it before making up your bag.

Fabric pen designs

There are a number of pens on the market now that provide you with great results, but you do get what you pay for. If they seem too cheap to be true, then they usually are. Using a fabric pen is very similar to using a standard felt-tip pen, and they give similar results. It's best to use lighter colours first; if you use a darker shade and then try to use a lighter one over it, the colours will mix and turn the lighter shade muddy. Once you've finished your design, leave it to dry and then iron over it to fix the dye into the fabric. Your design should be washable and colour fast, though you will experience some fading. Keep your pens handy to liven up the colours after a few washes.

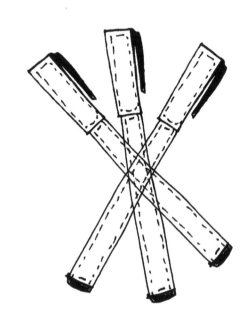

Appliqué

My favourite way of decorating totes is to use shapes of different fabrics to create a design. This not only gives an attractive result, but also makes a sturdier bag as you are, in effect, adding extra layers of fabric through your design.

Your design could be something as simple as a large letter, cut out of felt and sewn onto your bag, or as technical as a landscape scene made out of shades of green and blue fabric. As a rule, ensure your main fabric is a heavyweight, sturdy type; or, if not, use some interfacing to prevent the fabric gathering or pulling as layers are added.

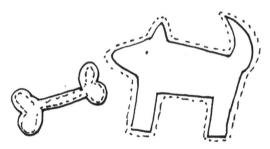

DECORATIVE BOW FOR A TOTE BAG

A large bow in a pretty fabric can instantly enliven a tote. Bows are a little involved to make but, once you've cracked it, you'll be able to make them for a host of projects.

You will need

One or two pieces of fabric to size of your choice

To make

1. Decide on the size of your bow and cut two pieces, remembering a seam allowance of 15mm all around. If you want to use the same fabric for back and front, simply cut a piece twice the width and fold in half.

2. Pin the fabric together, right side in and pin. Sew along three sides (or two if fabric is folded) and then turn right side out.

3. Fold in the open edge to disguise the raw edge of fabric and pin.

4. Cut another piece of fabric for the centre wrap around, measuring the width of your fabric by 45mm. Fold in the long sides 15mm, pin and sew in place.

5. Fold the wrap around the centre of the bow and pin in place at the back. Sew closed. The bow can now be used for decorating just about anything!

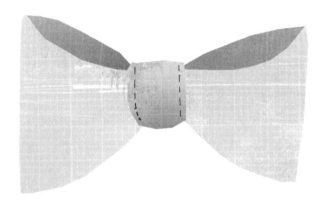

FELT SCALES/FEATHERS

This is a really easy and quick method of decorating your
bag, by creating a series of felt scales or feathers in the
colours of your choice. You can make the shapes as
large or as small as you choose and, if your patience
allows, you can decorate each individual scale with
embroidery and beads should you so wish. Again, attach
these before the bag is made up, as it won't be possible
after the seams are finished.

You will need

6–7 pieces of felt

Cardboard

To make

1. Choose your felt, using as many colours as you like, though around
   four to five works really nicely. Make a template from stiff card (as
   most children will tell you, a cereal packet will be perfectly adequate)
   using the shape shown as a guide. You can make them larger or
   smaller as you wish.

2. Use the template to count out how many shapes you can fit along the
   width of your bag; you want the shapes to fit closely together. Count
   out the number and add 1. Do the same along the length of your bag,
   but add 5. Multiply these figures together to give you the total number
   of shapes you will need to cut out. For example, if you can fit the
   shape on 6 times along the width, add 1 to give you a figure of 7. If
   you can fit the shape on 10 times along the length, add 5 to give you
   a figure of 15. Multiply 7 x 15 to give you a total number of 105 scales
   needed to cover the bag.

3. Cut the scales out of the different colours of felt. As felt does not need
   hemming, try and keep the scales as neat as possible.

4. Lay the first layer of scales along the base of the bag, keeping the
   bottom of the scales 5–10mm above the seam allowance at the base
   of the bag. Keep the scales as close together as you can without
   them overlapping. Pin them in place.

5. Sew the first layer to the bag, either by hand in one continual length
   of running stitch, catching all scales in place, or use the machine and
   straight stitch them into position.

Dragons?

Fishes?

Snakes?

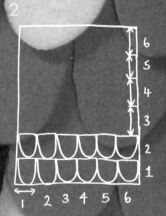

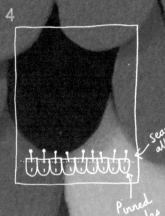

Seam allowance

Pinned Scales

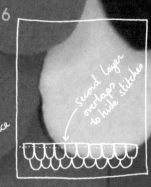

Second layer overlaps to hide stitches

6. Place the next layer onto the bag, hiding the row of stitches you have just made. Shift them across, so that the lower part of the scale is above the join of two below, similar to the design of bricks or roof tiles. Pin these in place and sew as for the previous layer.

7. Repeat the process until the bag is covered. If you wish, use a strip of fabric or thick ribbon to hide the stitches at the top of the final layer. Simply place this over the area to be covered, pin in place and sew into position neatly.

8. Make up the bag as before.

Why not try using different fabrics for the scales, either oversewing the edges to prevent fraying, or ironing on stiff interfacing to keep the threads together. You could use blues, purples and greens to make a trailing peacock's tail design; simply sew the scales onto a separate triangular piece of fabric and sew this onto the tote bag.

Altering the shape of a tote bag

The basic rectangle shape of a tote can be altered to produce something more interesting by modifying a few stitches at its base. Try sewing a semicircular seam at the base, rather than a straight edge, or (even easier) give the bag some depth by creating a base.

To do this, turn the bag inside out and lay it flat with the side seam in the centre as shown. Measure 30mm from the corner point and mark. Pin the corner flat and sew at 90° across the seam, at the point marked. Repeat at the other corner. This will flatten the base of the bag and provide you with a more professional look to your bag.

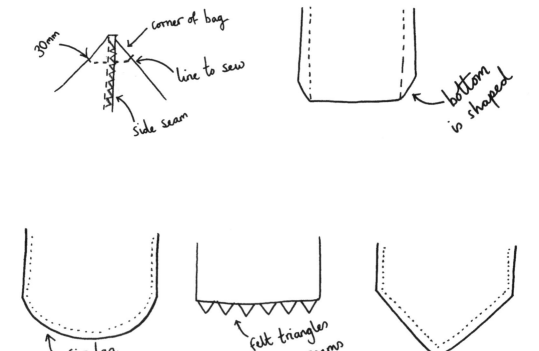

Lining your bag

This is an extremely simple way of strengthening (and adding a touch of decoration to) your tote bag. For lining, it is best to use a fabric that is much lighter in weight than the main body of the bag. Fabrics like thin cotton, silk, seersucker or thin linen are fine, or an old shirt or blouse will do the job nicely. It's best to add the lining to your bag after you have attached the handles.

To make

1. Cut out two rectangles of thin fabric, the same size as you have previously cut for your tote bag, including seam allowance.

2. Pin the edges together and sew along the two sides and bottom, taking care to leave 15mm seam allowance. If your lining is too small, it will be difficult to sew in; if it's too big, it is possible to ease it in by gathering the fabric in even sections.

3. Measure your bag and turn over the raw edge at the top to the correct depth. Press this flat.

4. Place the lining inside your tote. Pin the top of the lining in place, covering the raw edge of the main bag. Tack in place.

5. Either sew the lining in place by hand or by machine. If you use the machine and work with the lining top side up, make sure your top thread matches the lining and the bottom thread matches the bag. This will give you as invisible a seam as possible.

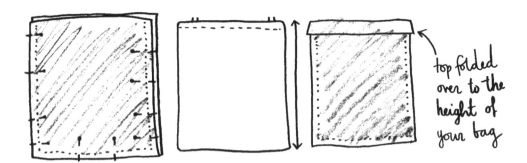

top folded over to the height of your bag

BASIC SATCHEL

This is slightly more involved than a tote bag in that in has a flap that folds over the top and fastens at the front. This basic design can be altered in a number of ways, most notably by using a soft leather and scaling up the design.

You will need

2000mm sturdy fabric, such as denim or tweed

2 D rings

A decorative button for the fixing

To make

1. Decide on the size of bag you wish to create and make the pattern up accordingly. You will need a large rectangle that will become the front, back and flap of the bag, and two smaller rectangles for the sides.

2. Cut the fabric and pin the sides to the front section as shown. Tack these together.

3. Fold the hem over along all three sections, press and pin. Sew this in place. If you are not going to line the bag, cover the raw edge of this hem by sewing a piece of ribbon over the top.

4. Pin the remainder of the sides to the back section of the bag and tack into place.

5. Fold the left hem of the flap over, press and pin, repeating with the right.

6. For the top hem, fold in the corners, as shown, press and then fold the top hem over the top. Press again to give a nice, clean finish to the hem. Again, if you are not lining the bag, the raw edge of the hem can be hidden with ribbon after applying the button flap.

7. Sew the bag together, starting at the front of one side, completing the full seam, then moving on to the hem of the flap. Follow this round, pivoting at the corners, then move on to the seam on the other side.

8. Unpick the tacking stitches and oversew the edges for a strong, neat finish. Turn the bag right side out.

2

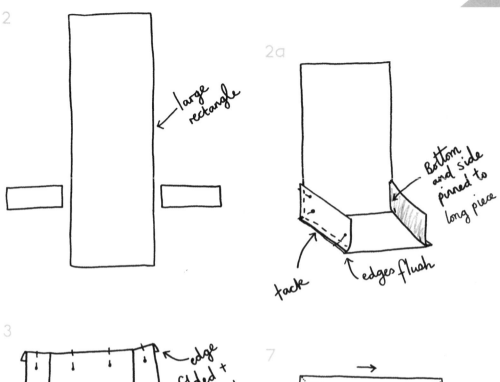

large rectangle

2a

Bottom and side pinned to long piece

tack

edges flush

3

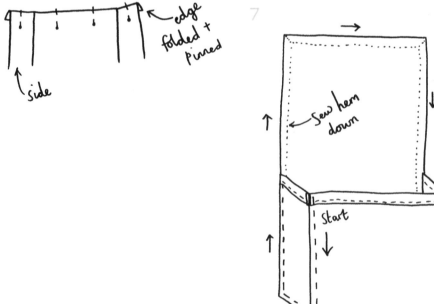

edge folded + pinned

side

7

Sew hem down

Start

End

9. To make the button flap, take two small pieces of fabric, roughly 35 x 60mm. Place them right sides together and pin. Hem the two long sides and one short. If you would prefer a pointed flap, sew at 45°, cutting off the corners at the short hem as shown. Turn this right side out and press. Pin in place behind the front flap directly in the centre.

10. If you wish to line the bag, repeat the process of making the basic satchel, using fabric of a lighter weight, without hemming the raw edges. Place the lining inside the bag, and fold in the seams, covering any raw edges and the button flap. Pin in place and hand sew the lining in, taking care to make the stitches as small and invisible as possible.

11. Make fabric loops for the D rings. Take a piece of fabric 45 x 120mm and fold the long sides in 10mm on each side. Press them flat and sew along the seams. Fold one short side over, press and sew in place. Make another loop with an identical piece of fabric.

12. Pin the raw edge of one loop in place as shown, with the right side face down, 30mm from the opening of the bag. Sew along the bottom of the loop. It may seem counter intuitive to sew with the right side face down, but this won't be seen when the bag is complete.

13. Thread the D ring onto the fabric loop and pin the neat edge to the bag, 45mm lower than the other join. Sew this in place in a rectangle, as shown, for stability. Repeat with the second loop.

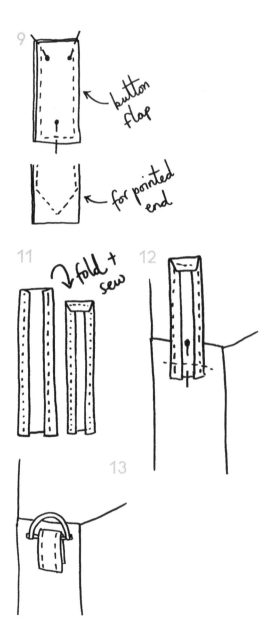

Making handles and straps for your satchel

There are a number of interesting options for handles. As for the basic tote bag, a man's tie is a good option, simply tied to each D ring, adjusted to your own preference. Another good option is to use an old belt, threaded through the rings and sewn in place for stability.

You can make your own strap using the same process as for the tote bag handles, with a larger width and length according to your preference. When your strap is complete, simply thread it through each D ring, fold the fabric back on itself to disguise the raw edge, and again to make a loop for the ring to sit within. Sew this using strong thread.

Using plastic handles

You can buy plastic handles from any craft shop that simply require you to sew a fabric loop through them. They give particularly professional results and provide an unusual design detail.

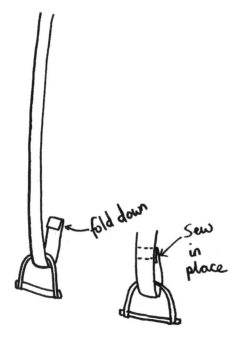

PLASTIC HANDLE HANDBAG

This bag is a perfect way of using up scraps of fabric. The shape of the body of the bag lends itself to a patchwork, as it doesn't need to be a perfect square. Here we have joined triangles of printed cloth, designed by textile artist Lu Summers. Her fabric has a beautiful doodled quality, and is all hand-screen-printed on oatmeal cotton.

Visit Lu's website at www.lusummers.co.uk

TURN THE PAGE FOR HOW TO!

You will need

A piece of fabric 500 x 1000mm (this can be a patchwork, wool, knitted, or whatever you like)

A piece of fabric 500 x 1000mm for the top (either to match, or contrasting)

Plastic handles

1 x 300mm zip

A piece of fabric 500 x 1000mm for lining

To make

1. Make your patchwork by connecting patches of fabric together as shown on page 62. You will need to create a piece of fabric that measures 500 x 1000mm.

2. Make the tops of the bag by cutting out two shapes as shown. The middle section should be just slightly less wide than the inside width of your plastic handle. Snip across the fabric as shown, folding in this edge and pressing flat. Sew these down.

3. Thread your handle onto the fabric and close the fabric around it. Pin in place. Sew the fabric along the side of the handle to keep it in place.

4. Fold over the bottom hems and press, tacking the seam in place, taking care only to sew one side at a time.

5. Open the zip and pin one side of the bag to the zip, as shown on page 71. Sew this in place. Repeat with the other side.

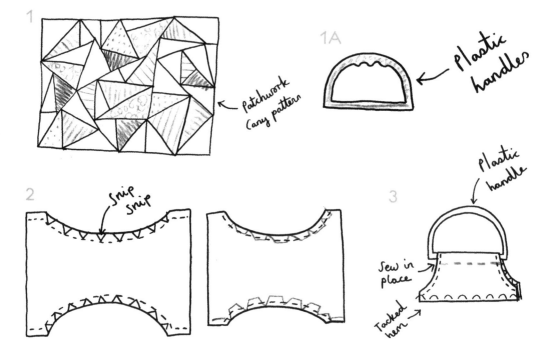

1

1A

Plastic handles

← Patchwork (any pattern)

Plastic handle

2

Snip Snip

3

Sew in place

Tacked hem

6. Complete the insertion of the handles by folding in the side seams. To hem the curve, snip the fabric as shown. Sew the hems together, hiding the raw edge and keeping the handle in place. Repeat with the other handle.

7. Take the patchwork fabric and fold it in half, right sides facing in, with the short sides together, and pin along the two side seams. Sew these closed using straight stitch and reinforce the seam by oversewing the raw edge.

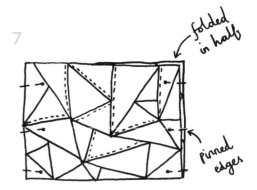

8. Shape the bottom by sewing the corners of the bag as shown on page 102 for tote bags.

9. Fold over the top raw edges of the patchwork fabric 20mm, creating a neat hem. Press this flat.

10. Repeat steps 7, 8 and 9 with the lining fabric.

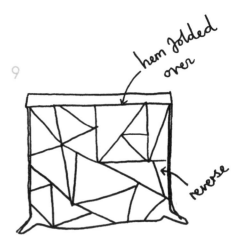

11. Working with the patchwork fabric right side in, pin your first fabric-covered handle to the bag. To do this, line up the bottom edge of the fabric with the raw edge of the hem of your patchwork. The handle should sit above the opening of the bag as shown. Repeat this with the second handle on the other side. Turn the bag right side out.

12. Place the lining (right side facing in) inside the patchwork bag. Line up the opening of the lining with the opening of the patchwork, effectively sandwiching the two fabric handles between the layers. Pin the patchwork, handle and lining together.

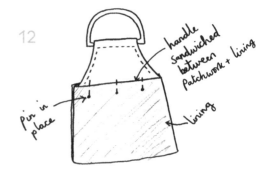

13. Sew the handles to the lining and patchwork, taking care that the handles remain in place.

VINYL LUNCHBAG

Mimicking paper bags, these are a very stylish alternative for transporting packed lunches, made from wipe-clean vinyl fabric (widely available from fabric shops). They can be made as large or as small as you wish, and even turned into a backpack with an alteration to the straps.

You will need

A piece of vinyl fabric 300 x 700mm

A decorative button

100mm cord or ribbon

Either 200mm (hand-held bag) or 1000mm (backpack) ribbon for handles

To make

1. Cut a piece of vinyl measuring 250 x 600mm.

2. Fold in half, right sides in, and sew along the two long sides using a sewing machine.

3. Flatten out the two sewn corners as shown and sew each at 90° to the seam, 40mm from the corner.

4. Run your fingers along the side seams to flatten them out, then turn right side out.

5. Flatten the base by folding along the corner between the side and the base. Repeat this on the other side.

6. Push in the side seams so the bag sits neatly. If you wish, to aid the bag in retaining its shape, simply sew along the corner lengths as shown.

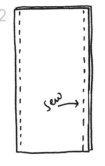

2

sew →

3

40mm

Corner

5

squeeze to fold bottom

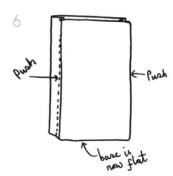

6

Push

Push

base is now flat

7. Fold over the entire top section at least 25mm from the edge. Sew a decorative button to the side on which the fold lies. Sew a loop of ribbon to the inside of the topmost layer, long enough to catch the button and keep the bag closed.

8. Make a handle using some thick ribbon, sewn to the opposite side from the button, as shown.

9. To make a backpack version for kids, measure how long they need the handles and make up the bag using a piece of vinyl measuring 300 x 800mm. Sew two pieces of ribbon as shown. The top sections should sit side by side along the centre of the top of the closed bag, with the bottoms in either corner.

7

fold in half + catch with a stitch

Sew ribbon loop

fold over

Sew button here

8

sew

handle version

9

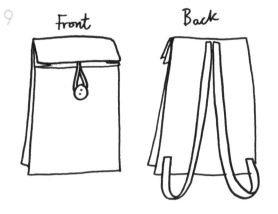

Front   Back

ONE-SEAM T-SHIRT BAG

This is possibly the simplest thing you will ever make, since T-shirt fabric doesn't fray in the same way as woven fabrics. Evoking the memory of the string bags popular in the 1950s and 1960s, these are great to leave in your car for supermarket runs. Using the basic shape of the T-shirt as a basis for the bag, simply make a few strategic cuts and close off the bottom hem.

You will need

An old T-shirt

To make

1. Use a clean, pressed T-shirt and begin by cutting away from the neckline, staying close to the top seams, but scooping down at the base as shown.

2. Cut off the sleeves, leaving at least 30mm at the top of the shoulder.

3. Turn the T-shirt inside out and pin the bottom hem closed. Sew this on the machine, creating a strong seam, using straight stitch and zigzig stitch over the edge.

4. If you wish to shape the bottom of the bag, fold in the corners as shown on page 102.

5. Using a fabric pen or chalk, mark a series of lines as shown on one side of the shirt. This is where you will slice into the T-shirt to make your expanding holes. The pattern should look a little like a brick wall. Repeat on the other side of the shirt.

6. Using sharp scissors, carefully slice into the fabric where your marks are. Don't make your cuts longer than the lines otherwise your shopping will fall through. Make sure you only cut through a single layer of fabric.

7. Turn the bag right side out and test the handles. If they feel too thick, take a long length of ribbon and tie it around the base of one of the handles. Wrap this around, covering the fabric, and tie off when you reach the other end. Repeat for the other handle.

Why not try using vests or old sweatshirts to make this bag. If you find it more comfortable, change the axis of the bottom hem so that the handles lie together.

1&2 Cutting Line

3 cut handles

pinned bottom hem

5 Snip Snip

snip lines

Keep them no larger than 30mm

7 tie ribbon round to strengthen + thin

LAUNDRY BAG

This can be made from an old sheet that has seen better days, which can either be left au naturel or dyed in the washing machine to your chosen colour.

You will need

An old sheet

2000mm cord

To make

1. Fold the sheet in half along the longer side. Pin together and sew along the bottom and side seams, stopping 200mm from the top.

2. Fold the top seam over 100mm and pin in place. Sew along the bottom edge, leaving a tube of fabric to house your cord.

3. Turn the right way out and thread the cord through the tube you have just made. If this is difficult, tape the cord to a knitting needle and use this to pull the fabric through the tube.

4. Gather the fabric along the cord and tie closed.

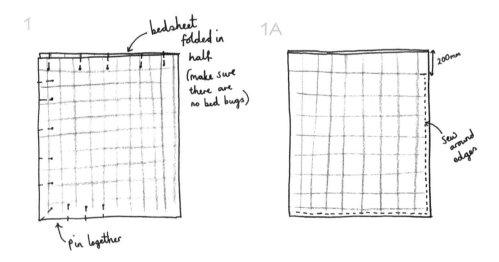

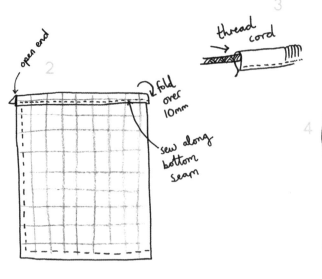

2

open end

fold over 10mm

sew along bottom seam

3

thread cord

4

also makes v. good Santa Sack

MAKE-UP ROLL

This is a very useful piece of kit for the ladies, which can be made as decorative as you like. A good tip is to use a piece of waterproof fabric (old cagoules are helpful here) as a lining to make sure your brushes and make up keep dry.

You will need

2 pieces of fabric 500 x 500mm

1 piece of interfacing 500 x 500mm

2 pieces of elastic 450mm long

500mm ribbon

To make

1. Cut out two pieces of fabric in contrasting shades measuring 500mm x 500mm and fold both in half lengthways, right sides in.

2. Pin and sew down both side seams as shown. Fold over the raw edges of one piece and press flat.

3. Turn right side out. Place one piece of fabric inside the other, hiding the raw edge as shown. Pin in place and sew along the seam.

4. Fold the bottom over, making a flap measuring roughly 150mm. Fold a piece of ribbon measuring 400mm in half and place between the fabric on the right. Pin the folds down and sew along each side.

5. Divide the roll into sections by sewing a row of stitches through all layers of fabric.

1   2   3

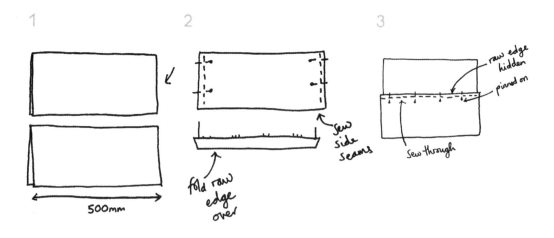

500mm   fold raw edge over   Sew side seams   raw edge hidden   pinned on   Sew through

Why not try using quilting, patchwork, appliqué or even woven ribbon to decorate your make-up roll. You can adapt many of the designs from other projects in this book.

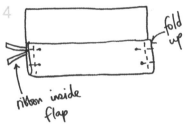

4

fold up

ribbon inside flap

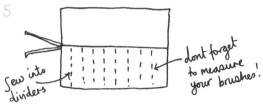

5

Sew into dividers

don't forget to measure your brushes!

BASIC MAKE-UP BAG/PENCIL CASE/WASHBAG

This design can be made smaller to create a pencil case, or larger, using waterproof fabric, to make a washbag. The bag consists of two identical rectangular pieces of fabric joined on three sides, with a zip on the fourth side to close it. You can make it from any fabric – denim, fleece, wool, fake fur or jersey – though for best results, it needs to be fairly thick.

You will need

A piece of fabric

1 zip

To make

1. For a pencil case, cut two pieces of fabric measuring 190 x 130mm. For a make-up bag, cut two pieces 200 x 160mm. To make a washbag you will need two pieces 300 x 270mm (don't forget to use waterproof fabric for this; an old shower curtain will work brilliantly).

2. Place both pieces of fabric side by side, face down, on a table. Fold over the top hem of both pieces 15mm and press. Repeat this, disguising the raw edge, and pin.

3. Take a zip measuring 160mm for the pencil case, 170mm for the make-up bag or 270mm for the washbag. Open it out as far as it will go and attach as shown on page 71 (the basic principle is the same).

4. Close the zip halfway and place both rectangles of fabric together, with right sides facing in. Be sure to line up the edges correctly. Pin and then sew along the three edges, lining up the seams with the edge of the zip.

5. Open the zip and turn the fabric the correct side out. Press the seams, using a pressing cloth if necessary.

2

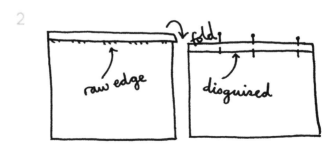

fold

raw edge

disguised

3

attach zip

4

zip half closed

wrong side

pin edges

seams

Making skirts

It really is possible to copy high-fashion designs using offcuts and recycled fabrics, especially if you keep things simple. The great thing about a skirt is that as long as it can be opened, and fits you at the waist and over your hips, a basic shape is all you need. So let's leave tailored designs to the professionals and let the floaty pieces rule.

THE EASIEST SKIRT IN THE WORLD

It truly is. If you use netting, it can be called 'the easiest tutu in the world'. The basic structure consists of a large tube of fabric gathered around an extremely thick piece of elastic. The trick is to make sure you can get the elastic over your hips (or shoulders, if you prefer to take the skirt over your head) without it being too loose at the waist.

You can make this skirt as full as you wish, simply by altering the amount of fabric you use. The more the merrier, I say. Also, if you choose a fabric such as jersey or T-shirt fabric, you may not need to hem the edge. Now that's what I call easy.

You will need

A piece of elastic 30mm (minimum) x 1000mm

A piece of fabric 2000mm in length

To make

1. Measure around your hips. Take this figure and double it. This is the length of fabric you will need.

2. Measure your waist. This figure will give you the length of elastic you will need. Use a minimum width of 30mm elastic, though you can go as wide as you like.

3. Now for the tricky bit. You need to stretch the elastic to the length of your skirt fabric, so that the fabric will ruche naturally and drape well. Pin the elastic 15mm from the long edge of the fabric, placing a pin at both ends, in the centre and at 400mm intervals. Put a couple of small tacks at these points to secure them. This will allow you to sew the elastic to the fabric a little more easily.

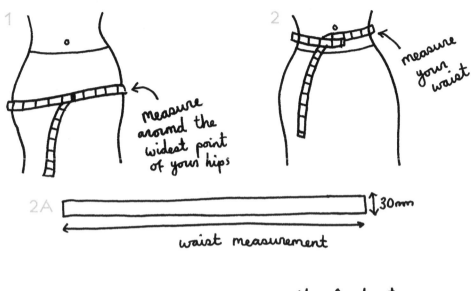

1

measure around the widest point of your hips

2

measure your waist

2A

30mm

waist measurement

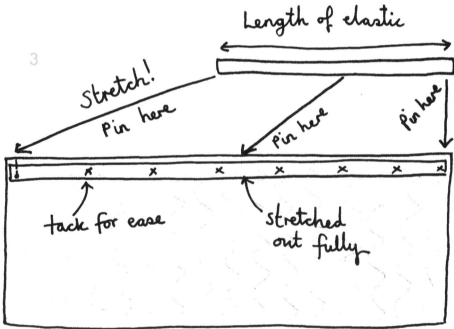

3

Length of elastic

Stretch!

Pin here

Pin here

Pin here

tack for ease

stretched out fully

4. Place the fabric under the sewing machine foot and bring the foot down. Grip the fabric at the end (mind your fingers) and the next tack point, and pull the elastic out so that the cloth underneath is flat. Begin sewing carefully, keeping the elastic taut throughout.

5. When you reach the next tack point, move your hands to pull the next section taut. Repeat the process until the elastic is fully sewn to the fabric.

6. Now you've done the hard bit, simply join up the open ends and pin together. You can sew down the width of the elastic and the seam of the skirt at the same time. Sew over the edge seam for strength and to neaten it off.

7. If your fabric needs hemming, simply fold in the raw edge, press and repeat, hiding the messy bits. Sew this closed – and go out and wear your skirt with pride.

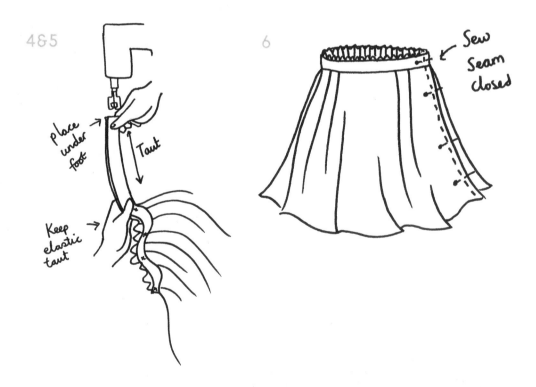

4&5

place → under foot

Taut

Keep → elastic taut

6

Sew Seam closed

use up old fabric in layers

Sew each layer to the previous one to make it easier to attach the elastic. For a fantastic 1950s-style outfit, make a netting version to wear under a single-layer skirt. Before you know it, you'll have a ra-ra skirt and a tutu for every occasion!

Why not try adapting the skirt by producing layers of fabric of differing lengths, as shown in the diagram.

THE SKIRT THAT USED TO BE TROUSERS

Rather than throwing away trousers with torn hems or the odd hole here and there, turn them into a neat skirt that will give you years of service. In fact, my favourite smart pencil skirt, worn to weddings, important meetings and evenings out, used to be a pair of pinstripe trousers.

This method works especially well with jeans, as you don't need to cut into the fabric much at all, leaving you with a rather chic denim number. You can cut the length to suit yourself, whether you want a calf-length skirt or a mini to wear over leggings, and choose between a thin pencil skirt or a more comfortable A-line style, simply by moving things out a bit. You'll find a seam ripper will make your life so much simpler when opening the inside seams.

You will need

A pair of old trousers

To make

1. Ensure the trousers are clean and pressed; it is really difficult to sew creased cloth.

2. Cut off the bottom hems 10mm higher than the seam. This will make it easier to get to the inside seams.

3. Using a seam ripper, open the inside leg seams right to the crotch. You may need to use scissors with jeans as they are usually held together very securely. Try and keep the face of the fabric clean by working slowly. It can be time-consuming, but it's worth it, I promise!

4. Unpick the seam just below the fly to open out the triangular shape. Repeat this on the back so that the fabric lies flat.

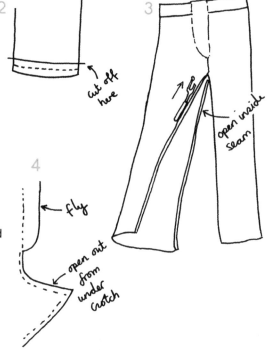

5. Lay the garment flat, with the triangular sections overlapping. If your trousers are denim, you can simply leave this shape intact. If not, you may want to cut this section straight. Decide on the length you want your skirt to be and mark, leaving a 15mm seam allowance. Cut off the excess fabric and save it; you will use this to fill the triangular section left in the skirt.

6. To make a narrow pencil skirt, pull the fabric across slightly, leaving a small triangular gap at the bottom of the skirt. Measure the gap and cut out a section of the excess fabric to fit. Try and keep the grain of the fabric running in the same direction.

7. For a wider, A-line skirt, pull the skirt open slightly. You will need more fabric to cover the hole, so bear this in mind when deciding on the length of your skirt. Measure the gap and cut out a section of the excess fabric to fit. Again, try and keep the grain of the fabric running in the same direction.

8. Place the section of fabric behind the gap and pin in place. Tack this down and remove the pins.

9. Sew the seams flat onto each other, and then join the added sections. You can either do this by hand or use your machine. If you would like to make the seams decorative, try using embroidery thread to oversew the edge using herringbone stitch. Alternatively, cover the seam with a length of decorative ribbon. Ensure you have sewn the front and the back.

10. Hem the bottom edge by folding it in 15mm, pressing and sewing closed. For a neater finish it's best to do this once your skirt has been constructed.

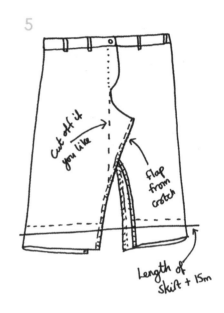

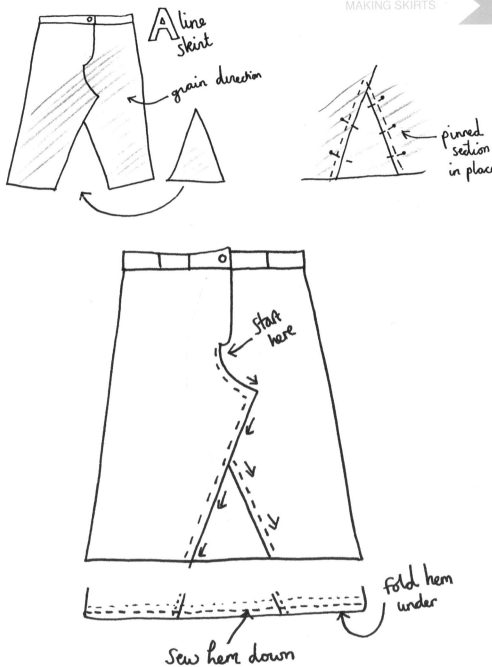

A line skirt

grain direction

pinned section in place

start here

fold hem under

Sew hem down

making household items

There are hundreds of things you can do for the home with recycled fabric.

BUNTING

A lovely addition to any party room, bunting is really easy to create and, if you make it from fabric, it is reusable. If you use felt, all you need to do is cut out the triangles and sew them to the tape. For an extra decorative finish you may want to use pinking shears. Chintz gives a really nice farmhouse effect and, if you ask your haberdashery for fat quarters of fabric, you can find a range of smaller pieces of cloth in different patterns to keep your costs down. For successful bunting, you need an even spacing of flags, leaving the gaps between them no larger than the width of one flag.

There are a number of ways of making your bunting. The easiest way is to use felt, which doesn't need hemming and is available in a range of cheerful colours. Cut out the shape using a stencil and sew the top edge to some thick ribbon or cotton tape. Try and alternate the colours for maximum impact.

Another way is to use two pieces of fabric, cut to shape, placed together (right sides in) and sewn along the two sides as shown. Turn the right way out and press flat. Repeat for all your flags. Sandwich your flags between two pieces of ribbon or cotton tape and sew together. This will give you really durable, reusable bunting.

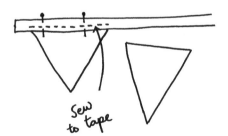

Sew to tape

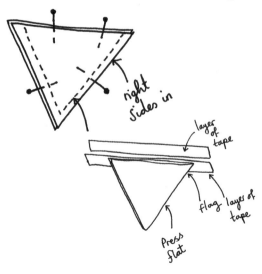

right sides in

layer of tape

flag layers of tape

Press flat

Why not try using waterproof fabric to make rainproof bunting that's suitable for the British summertime!

FELT GARLAND

This is a pretty and unusual alternative to bunting or tinsel, and you can make it in minutes. As it can be done by hand, and no hemming is needed, it's a great project to undertake with the children, as a fairly blunt needle will easily push through felt. (If you are enlisting the help of younger children, it's safer if you do all the cutting out yourself beforehand.) Pinking shears will give a decorative finish to the edges of each section.

You will need

3–4 pieces of felt

fold in half

sew onto one thread

To make

1. Choose a few colours of felt. Keeping to a limited palette of two to three colours works well, and the colours can be geared to your event (for instance, pinks for a girl's birthday, pastels for spring, red, green and gold for Christmas).

2. Using a jam jar as a guide (or the inner or outer edge of a roll of sticky tape), cut out a circular cardboard template. Place the template on your felt and draw round it with chalk or a fabric pen.

3. Cut out the circles using pinking shears. At least 20 shapes will give you a decent garland.

4. Thread a needle with embroidery thread in a complementary colour. Knot one end well, leaving at least 10mm excess thread. Take one circle and fold it in half. Thread your needle through the top of the semicircle, taking care to go through both layers of felt.

5. Using running stitch, sew in a straight line down the radius of the semicircle. When you reach the end, fold another circle in half and begin sewing through the top. Don't pull too hard, or the felt may not lie straight. The shapes should be just touching, with the thread acting as a central column. Repeat for all the other shapes.

6. When you have sewn all your shapes together, spread the shapes out so that they hang straight. Oversew a couple of stitches on the last shape and knot well to secure, leaving another 10mm excess thread. This will enable you to hang the garland from either end.

Why not try hanging some garlands as a lovely alternative to a window blind in a room where curtains are not necessary.

Simply make 10–12 garlands of differing lengths and attach one end of each to a piece of cane. The cane can be fixed to the top of the window using brass hooks. Thread the other end of each garland to a bead or button to act as a weight.

If you are feeling adventurous, why not make an extra large version of this as a door curtain? You could thread beads or bells in between your felt circles, to give a light jingle when the wind blows, as well as keep flies at bay.

TABLE RUNNER

This is another easy project, as in essence it is simply a rectangle of fabric with a weight at each end. This is a great opportunity for you to recycle those lovely tablecloths that have, alas, become holey or irrevocably stained. Or course, it is also a great opportunity to use a patchwork technique to create a unique design. And, if you've made it yourself, the family is guaranteed to take a little more care not to spill red wine over your handiwork.

The table runner can be as detailed or as simple as you wish. However, don't embellish it with beads or sequins, as hot pans may damage them and an uneven surface may cause cups and glasses to tip over.

You will need

2 pieces of fabric 2500 x 600mm

Any patchwork design

2 tassels (optional)

To make

1. Measure the length of your table. Decide if you would like the runner to stop before the table ends or run over the edges. Decide on a width for the runner; a popular choice is 450–500mm.

2. Cut two rectangular pieces of fabric to your chosen size. One will serve as the underside, one the top. If you have designed a patchwork for the top, make sure it is well pressed and hemmed. You may wish to sew this to a secondary piece of fabric that can be attached to the top of the runner.

3. Place your top and bottom fabrics together, facing inwards. Pin the edges together.

4. Sew along the long sides. Find the centre of the short sides and mark. You will also need to mark along each side seam 130mm from the corners. You will be joining both these marks to the central one to create your pointed ends.

5. Sew a line of stitches from the marks to the point, as shown, closing one end of the fabric. On the other end, sew from one mark to the centre only. This will leave you a gap through which you can turn the runner right side out. Press the runner flat. You may need to use a point turner or a stiff piece of card to get into the corners.

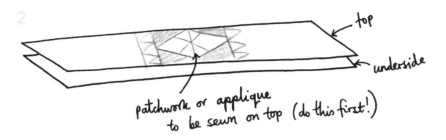

top

underside

patchwork or applique
to be sewn on top (do this first!)

3 & 4

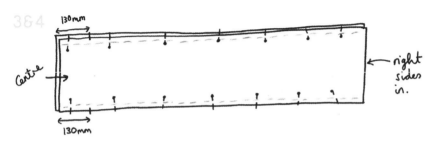

130mm

Centre

130mm

right
sides
in.

5

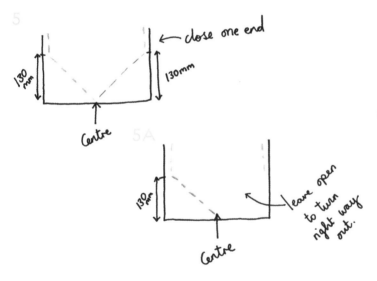

130mm

130mm

close one end

Centre

5A

130mm

leave open
to turn
right way
out.

Centre

6

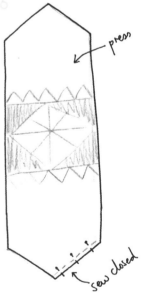

press

sew closed

6. Fold in the seam of the remaining open edge, press, pin and
tack closed. You may need to use slipstitch on this edge to
create an invisible seam.

7. If you wish to add a tassel or other embellishment to the points,
simply hand sew in place.

NO-SEW FESTIVE WREATH

A brilliant alternative to the traditional Christmas holly wreath, this has the added bonus of offering you a way of using up all those old pieces of fabric you've collected over the year. Intersperse larger pieces of fabric with some festive ribbon and, voilà, you've got a gorgeous wreath that is just too nice to leave outside.

You don't need to hem the fabric, as the frayed edges add to the wreath's charm.
To construct your wreath, you can use an old embroidery ring, a circular frame or (preferably) a polystyrene wreath template, available widely from craft shops and florists.

Alternatively, cut out a circle of cardboard and wrap some wool around it to strengthen and bulk out the template.

You will need

30–40 offcuts of fabric, at least 300mm long

10–20 lengths of ribbon, at least 300mm long

1 ring

1 piece of ribbon or string for the hanger

To make

1. Gather together a mass of fabrics. Measure the circumference of your template and add 200mm to this figure. This should give you the minimum length for each strip of fabric used.

2. Simply knot each strip of fabric around the template, leaving the sections loose as necessary. Try and keep the strips as close together as possible, interspersing them with ribbon as required.

3. To hang, tie a long piece of string or embroidery thread around the wreath and double knot. Make another double knot in the thread 100mm from the top of the template. You can now hang your wreath proudly from a nail or pin.

ring as template

keep tying!

AGA TOWEL

This is a great way of using towels that have seen better days. Don't worry if you don't have an Aga, these towels can hang over any oven door handle, or even over a bathroom towel rail. For a lovely country kitchen look, try teaming your towel with some floral-patterned cotton or linen. Wooden buttons or toggles look great with this type of fabric, though you can happily use any recycled buttons you may find at home.

Ideally the colour of your towel should influence your choice of fabric, though if you are using offcuts you may not have this luxury.

Do try and choose a fabric that will go in the washing machine without any problem, as a kitchen towel obviously needs regular washing.

You will need

1 towel

A piece of fabric 1000 x 600mm

2 decorative buttons

To make

1. Cut the top third off your towel. This could be an end that looks particularly tatty. If both ends look messy, cut them both off and hem one end.

2. Cut out a rectangle of fabric measuring 530mm x the width of your towel, plus a seam allowance of 15mm.

3. Lay the towel flat, with the raw edge at the top. Fold in the sides to the centre and pin in place.

4. Fold the fabric in half lengthways (i.e. with the long sides together), right side facing in, and pin the top and side edge. Sew along the pinned edges. Turn the raw edge at the bottom over as shown and press. Turn the fabric inside out.

1   Cut off top

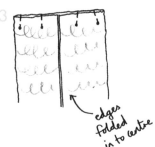

3   edges folded in to centre

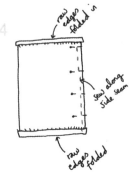

4   raw edges folded in   Sew along side seam   raw edges folded

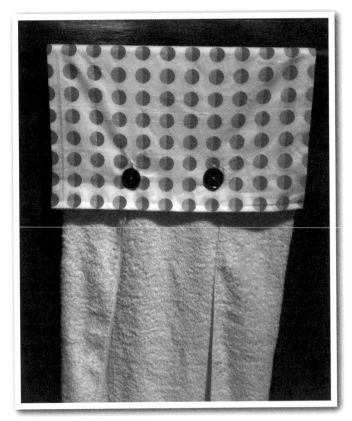

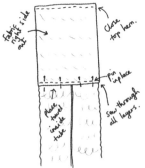

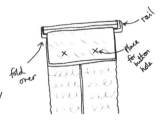

5. Place the folded towel inside the tube of fabric and pin 20mm from the raw edge. If you have a sturdy sewing machine, sew through all layers of fabric to secure the towel to the fabric. You will need to use a denim needle suitable for thick fabrics to ensure it does not break. If you're not happy about the strength of your machine, use a thick needle suitable for leather work (or even a bookbinding needle, which is sharp, thick and long) and sew by hand using strong thread.

6. Press the fabric and test where your buttons need to go by threading the fabric over the oven rail. Starting below the handle, feed the fabric end up and over. Line up the edge of the hem with the centre seam and mark two spots where the buttons will sit.

7. Sew on the buttons and make buttonholes in the correct places as shown on page 74. Your Aga towel is now ready for use!

making cushions

The beloved squashy square cushion is the best way of injecting a splash of colour and personality into a room without resorting to tangerine walls and intricate cornices. The simple shape allows you to go to town with the design, making your cushions as plain or as decorative as you like. Plus, there are masses of possibilities for recycling in their making. We'll start with a basic pad.

Filling

Whether you buy a ready-made cushion pad or fill the cushion yourself (avoid dried pasta – it really doesn't work), the filling can make a surprisingly big difference to the look of your cushion. Feather fillings provide a luxurious, though allergenic, filling (bear this in mind if your cushion is a gift). They can also look a little flat so, if you want a plumper cushion, try some artificial wadding.

CUSHION PAD AND NON-REMOVABLE COVER

Cushion pads are really useful and inexpensive, and are readily available from haberdasheries and high street homewear stores.

They usually come with a label giving information about their fire retardant qualities, so make sure you buy one that includes this information. You can purchase a cushion pad for under £3, making the recycled fabric cushion a wonderfully inexpensive gift. The pads come in a range of sizes, usually from 10 inches (25cm), and are available in synthetic or feather varieties. I usually go for a pad rather than simply stuff the cushion myself, especially if I am making it as a gift. However, you can use the contents of an old pillow, soft toy stuffing, rags, wool or cushion foam to stuff your cushion.

You will need

2 pieces of thin fabric 500 x 500mm

Filling

To make

1. Decide on the size of your cushion. The standard size is 350–400mm, but you can go as big or small (or rectangular) as you require. Using thin cotton (or even interfacing – you will be covering the pad so this is just a structural requirement), cut out your chosen shape, leaving a 15mm seam allowance.

2. Pin the fabric together and sew along three sides. Continue to sew along the fourth side, stopping halfway along. This is the hole through which you turn the bag inside out and stuff the cushion.

3. To stuff the cushion you can use wadding from a pillow or old cushion, rags, feathers, offcuts of fabric or even old ribbon, bearing in mind that rags or offcuts will not give you as smooth or comfortable a finish as wadding or stuffing would. Make sure everything is clean before you use it. Simply fill the bag until the hole is gaping slightly, but still closes easily.

4. Fold in the raw edges of the fabric and oversew the edge by hand to close the cushion. Your cushion pad is now ready for its cover.

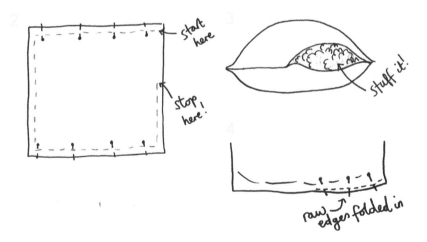

To make a non-removable cushion cover

1. Measure the cushion pad using a tape measure and cut two pieces of decorative fabric to fit, plus an extra 25mm both sides and 15mm seam allowance. If you wish to use the same fabric for both sides, simply cut one piece double the width and fold in half. Fabrics such as printed linen, velvet, tartan, tweed or a shiny venetian are great for this.

2. Place right sides in together and pin. Sew three sides closed (or two sides if fabric is folded) and trim any excess fabric. Trim the corners by snipping off a triangle 45° from the fabric edge.

3. Turn the right way out and turn in the raw edges of the final open side. Press the cushion cover flat.

4. Place your cushion pad inside the cover and pin the open end closed. Using slipstitch or a decorative blanket stitch (it's up to you if you take it the whole way round the cushion) close the cushion.

Removable cushion covers

It is sometimes preferable to have washable covers, in which case you need to be able to remove the cushion pad (as they don't wash well). There are a number of methods for closing your cushion, all fairly simple to finish. Let's begin with the most common – a zip closing.

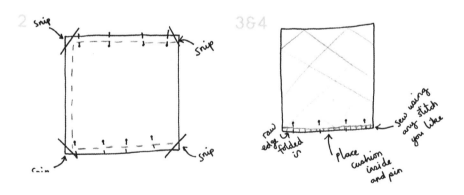

ZIP-CLOSED CUSHION COVER

You will need

2 squares of fabric big enough to cover your cushion pad

1 zip

To make

1. Cut out the fabric to fit your cushion pad, leaving a 20mm seam allowance. Fold over the top hem of both pieces and pin in place separately. Sew this in place and repeat, so the raw edge of the fabric is disguised.

2. Using a zip that is the length of the finished cushion (not including seam allowance), open it out and pin it in place to the hemmed edges of both pieces of fabric as shown. Place the top of the zip at the mark of the seam allowance (i.e. not at the edge of the fabric). Ensure the zip is 2–3mm lower than the edge of the hem, as this will hide the zip when it is closed.

3. Tack the zip in place, remove the pins and then machine sew the zip in place (see page 71 for more details).

4. Close the zip halfway and pin the fabric together, right sides in, being careful to line up the sides. The ends of the zip should mark the seam line.

5. Sew the other three sides closed. Trim the excess fabric and snip off the corners.

6. Turn the cushion the right way out, insert your cushion pad and close the zip.

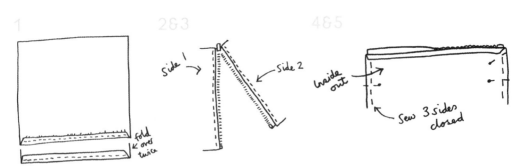

BUTTON-CLOSED CUSHION COVER

This looks fantastic if you use a plain fabric and decorative buttons. Try a biscuit-coloured linen with large magenta buttons. Lovely!

You will need

A piece of fabric 2000mm in length

2 decorative buttons

To make

1. Cut out a 580mm square of your fabric and a rectangle measuring 580 x 880mm. The larger piece will form your button flap.

2. Pin a 20mm hem on one short side of your rectangle and sew it closed. Repeat this to disguise the raw edge of the fabric.

3. Fold this edge back on itself, right side facing in, with the fold 150mm from the hem edge. Pin the edges of the flap.

4. Pin a 20mm hem on one side of your square of fabric and sew it closed. Repeat to disguise the raw edge.

5. Lay your rectangle flat, with the right side facing up. Place the remaining square of fabric with the right side facing down, lining up three edges with the three remaining raw edges of the rectangle. Pin together.

6. Starting at the top right-hand corner of the flap, sew along the edge, carrying on to the cushion body. Pivot at the corners, sew along the base and continue up the remaining side. This will sew the main cushion and the flap in one continuous line of stitches.

7. Turn the cushion and the flap right side out. Iron flat.

8. Decide where the buttons will go (no further from the opening than 100mm) and mark with a piece of chalk. Sew the buttons to the main body of the cushion as shown on page 74 and close the flap. Mark where the buttonholes are to go and create them following the instructions on page 74.

9. Place the cushion pad inside the cover and button closed.

Why not try altering this pattern to make a diagonal flap, with a single button at the centre

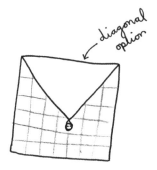

diagonal option

For this option, simply sew two diagonal lines to make a point on the flap, after completing step 6 above. A small loop of cord or ribbon attached at the point will remove the need for creating a buttonhole for closing.

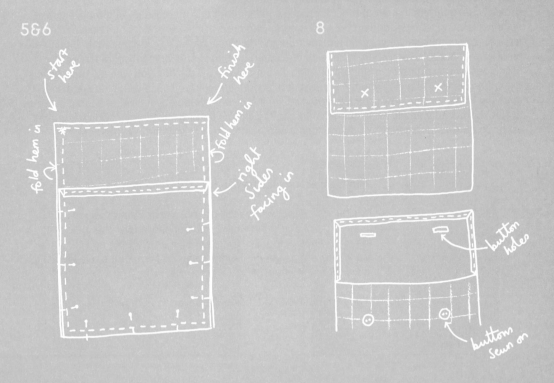

5&6

start here

fold hem in

finish here

fold hem in

right sides facing in

8

button holes

buttons sewn on

Decorating your cushions

Just as with tote bags, there are so many ways to decorate your cushion, it is impossible to fit them all in here. Once you have mastered creating a plain cushion, you can adapt it using appliqué, patchwork (recycling any scraps of fabric you may have collected), fabric pens, or even investing in a screenprinting course to generate your own printed patterns for soft furnishings. Courses are available throughout the country, suitable for all abilities. Look on the Internet for your nearest print studio. However you decide to decorate your cushion, though, it's always best to decorate each side before making up the cushion.

Get the children involved

Ask your children to draw a design on a light fabric (such as cotton or linen) using fabric pens. When they have finished, choose some matching embroidery thread and, using backstitch, sew along their lines for a permanent doodle.

Sourcing on the Internet

eBay is a brilliant resource for finding unusual fabrics to use in your projects. You can purchase scraps or fat quarters that are perfect for patchworking or for use in appliqué. Alternatively, why not try searching for independent print designers, who create unusual and unique designs for fabrics. You can usually buy fabric directly from the designer, giving you the opportunity to create products not available anywhere else, with the added benefit of supporting local artists. The online designer/maker stores Not on the High Street or Etsy will provide you with a direct link with the artists, as well as giving you the safety net of secure shopping. These websites are also a fantastic way of seeing new products and discovering new techniques you like, encouraging you to give them a go yourself. You can also purchase patterns for projects directly from designers, either as downloadable PDFs or as traditional paper items sent to you through the post.

Using collections of buttons

Buttons are a fantastic way of quickly decorating plain fabric. You can also use them to cover stains on cushions you already own. If you separate your collection of buttons into different colours, you can quickly amass a range of lovely pieces that will enliven any item.

BUTTON AND PLEAT CUSHION

This design is one of my favourites and can be produced in any colour. I tend to use crêpe-backed satin for the bulk of the cushion as it is reversible and enables you to change textures without changing the colour. You could do the same with any fabric that has a slightly different underside. If you don't have much fabric, let your buttons dictate the colour of your cushion; if you have a glut of green buttons, use green fabric, or a complementary colour such as purple or magenta. If you have a piece of fabric you wish to use, you can buy pots of different buttons from fabric mill shops, or (as usual) eBay can help with cheap offerings.

TURN THE PAGE FOR HOW TO!

You will need

A piece of fabric

Collection of buttons

600mm ribbon

To make

1. Cut out two squares of fabric 580 x 580mm. There's little point in making a smaller version, but of course, it's up to you. Set one piece aside.

2. Cut a further two pieces, one 150 x 600mm (piece A) and another 300 x 900mm (piece B). Decide which side of the fabric you would like to have as the main cushion.

3. Take piece A and, working with the right side as the opposite to the main cushion, fold the long sides over 15mm and press.

4. Take piece B and pin the short edge to the main cushion, lining up the pieces in a corner.

5. Pleat the fabric using knife pleats as shown on page 77. Try and keep the pleats equidistant, with each fold line 30mm from the next. This should give you around 10 folds. Remember to pin, tack and press the pleats in place to ensure the best results.

6. Secure the pleats by pinning a 300mm piece of ribbon (at least 15mm in width) in a harmonious colour over the raw edge of one side of the pleats. Sew along both lengths of the ribbon. Do not remove the tacks until the cushion has been made up.

7. Pin piece A over the other raw edge of the pleated section, this one running through the entire width of the cushion. You may wish to place this at a slight angle (as shown). Sew this in place, joining both edges of the strip. You will now have three sections marked on the cushion.

8. In the smaller section next to the pleats, lay your buttons out, filling as much of the section as you can. Try and leave 20mm from the seam edge, as they may interrupt you while you are sewing the cushion together. Using the technique shown on page 74, sew the buttons on securely.

9. Make up the cushion as shown in either the non-removable or zip-closed cover versions already shown.

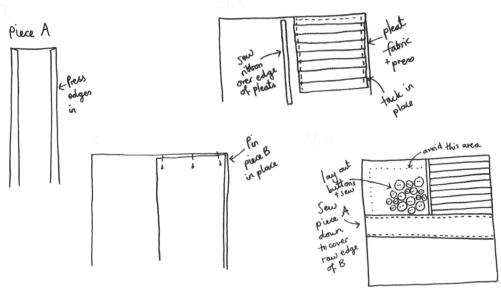

Piece A

← Press edges in

Sew ribbon over edge of pleats →

pleat fabric + press →

tack in place

← Pin piece B in place

avoid this area →

lay out buttons + sew →

Sew piece A down to cover raw edge of B

making curtains

The difference in price between buying curtains for your house and making them yourself can be immense. Your local haberdasher will always have a bargain rolls section, where you can buy wide fabric for under £2 a metre. Considering that ready-made curtains may cost you £50–£70, you could make some beautiful ones yourself in the fabric of your choice for a tenth of the cost.

UNLINED CURTAINS

Unlined curtains are extremely easy to make, as they are constructed from a rectangular piece of fabric, double hemmed, with curtain heading tape attached at the top. If you want to make unlined curtains that will still block out the light, choose a heavyweight fabric that will do all the work for you. If your main aim is merely to prevent others from being able to see into your home, choose a light linen or muslin fabric that will provide privacy while allowing a flood of light to be diffused through into your room.

You will need

At least 4000mm curtain fabric

The same amount of lining fabric (optional)

3500mm curtain header tape

To make

1. Measure your window. This seems an obvious starting point, but it is very important; estimating the size of something so large is notoriously difficult. Make sure you're clear about what you want. For instance, do you want two curtains that just meet in the middle; or do you want a large amount of fabric at the window, so that your curtains don't need to stretch too far to close? When you have decided on the size of each curtain, cut one or two pieces as needed, including a seam allowance of 80mm.

2. Press the curtain. This will make it easier to deal with.

3. Place the curtain right side down on a table or clean floor. Fold in the side seams 20mm and pin. Sew these in place. Repeat, giving you a double seam that hides the raw edge.

4. If you wish to use a curtain weight, place this 20mm from the raw edge of the bottom of the fabric. Fold the hem over, catching the weight, and pin. Sew this in place and repeat, providing you with a double hem. Press the hem flat.

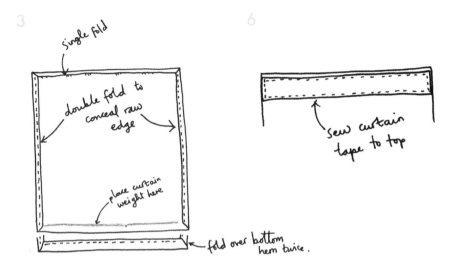

5. Fold over the top hem, pin, sew into place and press. You don't need to double hem this edge, as the curtain heading tape will disguise the raw edge.

6. Cut a length of curtain heading tape to the width of your hemmed curtain. Pin in place, and sew along the top and bottom edge. Repeat with the second curtain.

To make lined curtains

There is very little difference between lined and unlined curtains. In both cases, the hems are turned in twice to disguise the raw edge. The lining material should be much lighter than the curtain itself, and is usually in a cream or ivory colour. Simply cut a piece the same size as your curtain and press the fabric. Place it directly on top of your curtain with the right side facing out. Keeping the fabric together, simply repeat steps 3–6 of the instructions for unlined curtains.

making blinds

RAINDROP ROLLER BLIND

Tired old roller blinds can be rejuvenated with a spot of judicious appliqué. You can use any design that takes your fancy, but this one allows you to pull down a pretty cloud when the real ones gather ominously outside. This works particularly well when the blind is permanently pulled halfway down. The beaded raindrop fringe will provide added privacy, while allowing a little more light through.

You will need

1 plain white, cream or blue roller blind

A piece of fabric 1000 x 500mm

Embroidery silk

40–50 beads or buttons

To make

1. Measure halfway up the window. This will give you the height of your cloud. The width of the blind, less 20mm either side, will give you the width. Make a template out of thin cardboard, using the drawing as a guide.

2. Choose blue or grey fabric. Gingham or floral chintz will give a very pretty effect. The fabric should not be too thick, as you will need to iron on some light interfacing to prevent the edge from fraying. Using a cool iron, press the interfacing onto the back of the fabric. Use the template and draw the cloud (in reverse) on the back.

3. Cut out the strengthened fabric and pin 20mm from the hem of the roller blind.

4. Using the appliqué stitch of your choice, attach the motif to the blind by hand, using a thick chenille needle and embroidery thread to match.

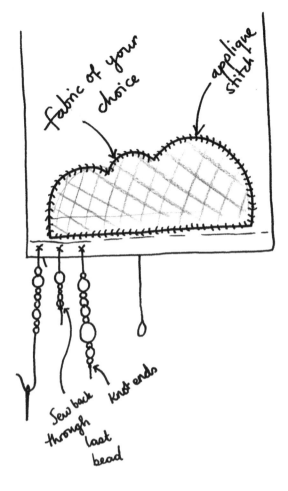

fabric of your choice

applique stitch

Sew back through last bead

Knot ends

To make a beaded fringe

You can add as many or as few raindrops to your cloud as you wish. It works best if the droplets are of differing lengths. Glass or metallic beads will give a nice effect as the light reflects off them.

1. Thread a skein of embroidery thread onto a thick needle and make a large knot on the end. Working from the reverse of the blind through to the front, sew 30mm from the edge of the cloud, pulling the thread through until the knot stops you. Sew a small cross to secure, bringing the thread out through the centre of the cross.

2. Thread on 10 or 12 beads, finishing with a small button. Sew through the holes a few times before pushing the needle through the threads as shown. Trim the thread.

3. Repeat this 30mm to the left with another 15–20 beads, and again 15mm to the left with 5–8 beads, and so on. Making the distances between the strands of beads uneven gives a more natural effect.

Creating personalised gifts

HANGING BIRD DECORATION

This is a very easy project that can be done entirely by hand. It makes a particularly attractive gift, especially as a Christmas ornament for a newborn baby. You can alter the shape and design to anything you like, and if you sprinkle in a little dried lavender with the stuffing, it can even be used to keep clothes smelling heavenly. You can use any fabric you like, but felt will be the easiest for your first one.

You will need

3–4 pieces of felt in different colours: for this bird decoration, you will need yellow, red, green and orange

Wadding for stuffing

Buttons or beads for eyes

Ribbon for hanging the decoration

Embroidery silks

To make

1. Using the drawing shown, make a template and cut out the basic shape of the bird from your base colour.

2. Cut out the elements, such as the wings and the beak, to build up the detail of the bird. Using embroidery thread, sew the elements onto one side. Repeat them on the other side.

3. Cut a piece of ribbon 140mm and fold in half to make a loop. Pin between the two pieces of fabric as shown. Tack this in place.

4. Place both sides of your bird together and pin, right sides facing out. Using blanket stitch, sew along the outer edges, leaving a gap of around 300mm.

5. Fill your bird with wadding (or stuffing of your choice – leave the Paxo for the kitchen, though!). When it is sufficiently plump, continue sewing in blanket stitch to close the gap. Be careful to ensure the ribbon loop is not tucked in.

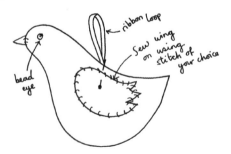

RECYCLED FABRIC COASTERS

This is a decorative, useful way of using up tiny scraps of fabric.

You can use any fabrics you have to hand, though try to keep them a similar weight. If they are mainly heavyweight items, simply place the fabrics side by side and sew them together using herringbone or cross stitch over the raw edges. One side of the stitch should pick up one fabric and the other side the next. Place lighterweight fabrics face down on an ironing board (or, if space is an issue, a folded towel on a table top) as close together as possible. If you have any gaps, simply cut pieces to fit from excess fabric. In both cases, try and fill a space 300 x 300mm, as it is easier to cut the pieces square from a larger piece than to create individual shapes. Place a piece of medium interfacing, glue side down, on the wrong side of your shapes and iron on well. Then, turn them over and either hand sew over the raw edges with decorative stitches, or place ribbon across the joins and sew it into place.

You may wish to spray your finished coasters with a Scotchguard fabric protector or water repellent to protect them against the odd spill of tea or coffee. You can buy this from most DIY or furniture stores or, alternatively, it may be more cost-effective to purchase it online.

You will need

A mass of scrap fabrics

Piece of felt for backing

Interfacing

To make

1. Cut the fabric you have created (or another larger piece of your choice) into pieces 100mm square (square A). Cut a piece of felt for the back of the coaster 80mm square (square B).

2. Using square A, fold over the edges 10mm, pin and press. Sew round the entire edge of the square.

3. Place square B, right side out, in the centre of square A. The edge of square B should touch the raw edge of square A.

4. Fold over the four protruding sides of square A, hiding the raw edge of square B. Pin in place and tack to secure.

5. Sew along the entire outside edge to secure in place.

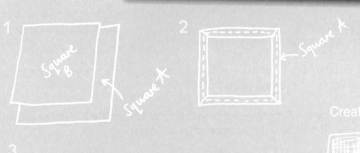

1

Square B

Square A

2

Square A

3

Sew in place

felt backing

Creating your fabric

stitch over edges

create your fabric

SUZANNE HARULOW'S FABRIC WALL HANGING

This project is the inspiration of textile artist Suzanne Harulow, founder of skybluesea, a creative company that uses 'rescued' clothing, buttons and jewellery to produce beautiful artworks and gifts. It uses recycled denim, linen buttons and jewellery to make a stunning wall hanging.

Suzanne blends a mix of hand-stitched details with items personal to her clients, such as lace from a christening gown, beads from a wedding dress or buttons from a shirt worn for a successful job interview, to produce truly unique pieces. This wall hanging makes a wonderful gift (especially for weddings, special birthdays or anniversaries) if you use similar elements that have special meaning for your recipient.

The design uses the textures and seams of rescued denims as part of the design, so don't be afraid of using sections that have been joined together. For additional contrast, use the reverse of the denim.

You will need

1 rescued denim pocket and/or 8–10 pieces of blue, cream and pink fabrics, all roughly 100 x 150mm (for appliqué)

Objects you have found

Fabric paint (dark colour, preferably)

Paintbrush

Alphabet stamp set

15–20 decorative buttons

1 piece of denim measuring 170 x 270mm

1 piece of denim measuring 170 x 80mm for the top

1 piece of contrasting fabric for the reverse, measuring 170 x 270mm

Jewellery wire for the handle, 500mm in length

Embroidery thread

Sewing machine

Denim needle

Awl

Ensure all pieces of fabric are pressed before use

To make

1. Create your design for the front of your wall hanging. It's best to have a small sketch to refer to. Work in layers on the largest section that will be sewn to the base. Assemble your design by cutting each element out from your chosen fabric. In the case of the beach hanging, the roof of the beach house is denim, with a linen wall and a button window; in the other, a denim pocket has been used for storing treasures.

2. Simply tack your piece in place where you want it to go and secure it around the edge using the zigzag function on your machine. You can use any of the appliqué stitches to secure your design, as shown on page 98.

3. Lay your piece of denim out on a table and lay your design in place. In this case, it is placed 50mm from the top and approximately 25mm from either side. Pin in place and sew on, using the stitch of your choice.

4. To make your label, choose a light-coloured fabric and cut out a section at least 100 x 800mm. Decide on the word you wish to use and paint the fabric paint onto the rubber section of the stamp. Practise on a scrap of similar fabric to see how the fibres take the paint. Once you are happy with the effect, print your work onto your fabric. Leave to dry according to the instructions on your pot. When dry, trim to 6mm away from the edge of your fabric and sew onto your wall hanging.

5. Sew on your found object (in this case, a small piece of driftwood) by securing it at strategic points, using a full six strands of embroidery thread. Knot well on the reverse of the fabric.

6. Place the front of the wall hanging together with the backing fabric, right sides facing in. Pin the edges and sew along the right, bottom and left seams. Turn right side out and press along the edges, taking care to avoid your precious items.

7. To finish the top, take another piece of denim and use the reverse as the right side. Fold in the two shorter sides 15mm and press. Repeat with the two longer ones. Pin this in place on your wall hanging, covering the raw edge at the top. Sew along the length, securing the fabric.

8. To make your wire hook, make two small holes in your fabric using an awl or thick needle. Fold the wire in half to give a double layer. Feed one end through your hole, pushing around 60mm out the other way. Wrap this around itself as shown.

9. Thread the buttons onto both strands of wire. Push the open end of the wire through the opposite hole and secure.

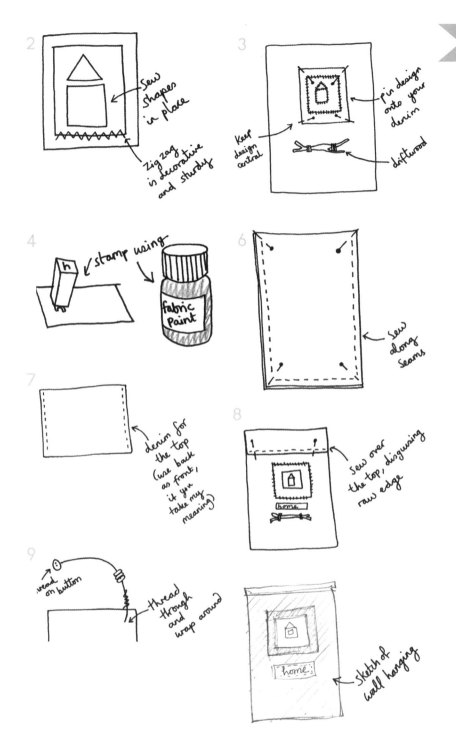

2

Sew shapes in place

Zig zag is decorative and sturdy

3

Keep design central

Pin design onto your denim

driftwood

4

stamp using

fabric Paint

6

Sew along seams

7

denim for the top (use back as front, if you take my meaning)

8

Sew over the top, disguising raw edge

home

9

thread on button

thread through and wrap around

home

Sketch of wall hanging

CHRISTMAS STOCKING

This is extremely easy to create, and again makes a wonderful gift for a new baby, as it can be kept year after year. Christmas stockings can be very expensive to buy, so making them yourself is an economical option.

You can use any fabric, in any colour, and make the stocking as decorative or as plain as you like. It's also up to you what size you make it, though a length of 500mm will serve you well.

In this design we have used pockets taken from old clothes, to make more room for extra little gifts. If you can't find any old ones to use, follow step 4 to make them from recycled pieces of fabric.

You will need

A piece of fabric 1200 x 1000mm

Offcuts of fabric

100mm length of ribbon or cord

Recycled pockets

To make

1. Using the template, cut two pieces from a thick fabric (ideally, red velour!). If you are cutting from a bought fabric, fold the fabric down the centre, right side facing in, and cut through two layers. If you are using two separate fabrics, make sure one is a mirror image of the other, as your shape will not work otherwise.

2. Cut out the accent colours for the top, heel and toe in felt or another fabric that doesn't fray. Pin these to the front of the stocking and sew in place.

3. Pin on a recycled pocket halfway up the stocking and sew along the two sides and bottom seam, leaving the top section open for tiny presents.

4. If you haven't got a recycled pocket, you can easily make one using a rectangle of fabric. Choose a festive fabric that complements the main colour of your stocking. You can make the pocket any size you want, though 50 x 80mm will work well. Fold the top seam over 10mm and press for a straight, neat edge. Repeat this fold to hide the raw edge. Sew the hem in place. Fold over the remaining seams 5mm and press. Pin the pocket to your stocking and sew in place.

5. Fold over the top 10mm of the hems of both pieces of the stocking and press. Repeat this fold to disguise the raw edges and sew in place.

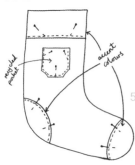

1&2

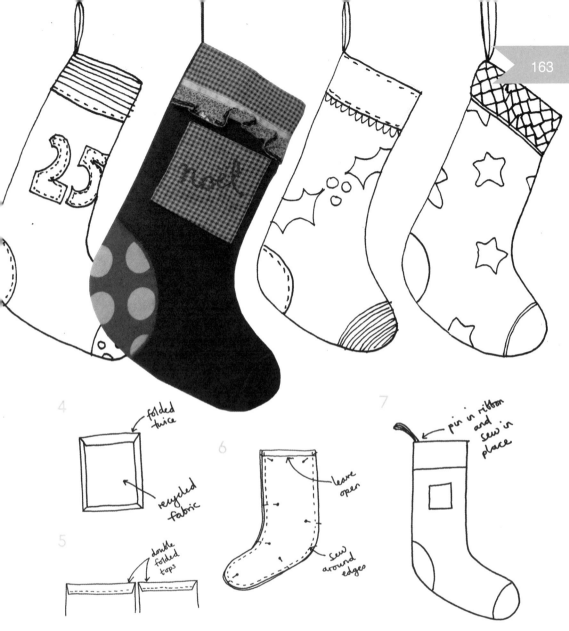

6. Place the two sections of the stocking together, right sides in, and pin. Sew along the outer edge, leaving the top open, ready for presents! You may wish (and need, if the presents are heavy) to oversew the seam for strength and neatness.

7. Take your length of ribbon, decorative cord, or a strip of fabric, fold it in half to make a loop and pin this into the inside seam (before you sew up the seams). Sew it in place securely, as this is how you will hang the stocking from the fireplace. This works best if you place the ribbon on the side opposite to the toe.

RECYCLED SKIRT APRON

This is a great way of dealing with skirts that no longer fit or are a little bit tatty, and there is very little sewing involved. The apron works best if made from a skirt that's quite full and flared, to give maximum protection to your clothes from accidents in the kitchen. Ensure the skirt is washed and pressed before you alter it.

You can also make this from scratch using the fabric of your choice by simply cutting out each piece, making the waistband as you would create a handle for a bag, and hemming the sides.

You will need

One skirt, at least 400mm long

2000mm length of ribbon, 30mm wide

To make

1. Lay your skirt out flat on a table. If the skirt has a zip or button opening, place this at the back. If your skirt has an elastic opening, place the seam to the back. If there are two seams, place these at the sides.

2. Cut along each side, slicing straight through the waistband as shown. Fold over the side edges 15mm, press and pin down. Sew these hems in place. Repeat this to disguise the raw edge.

3. Cut out a shape as shown from the remaining fabric, measuring roughly 275 x 330mm. Fold over the top edge, press, pin and hem. Do this for the sides and repeat to disguise the raw edges. Pin the bottom edge behind the waistband of the skirt and sew in place.

4. Cut two pieces of ribbon 600mm long and pin at either side of the waistband. Sew this in place and trim the edges with one (or two) diagonal cuts for neatness.

5. Use the remaining 800mm to make a loop at the top of the apron. Pin one end to a corner, lay it around your neck and pin the other end at the correct height for comfort. Sew this in place.

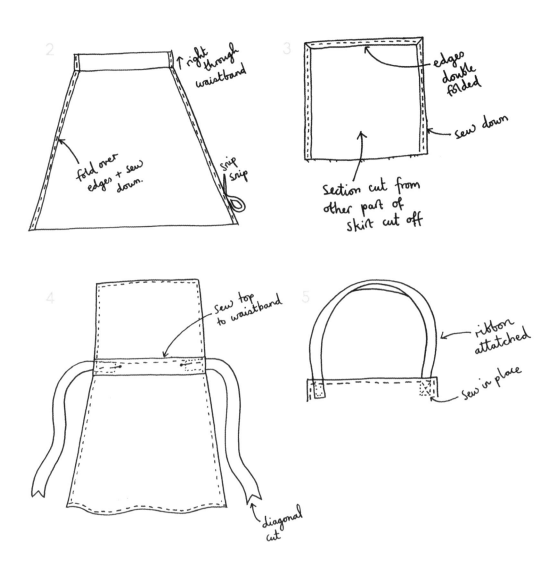

2 ↑ right through waistband

fold over edges + sew down.

snip snip

3 edges double folded

sew down

Section cut from other part of skirt cut off

4 sew top to waistband

diagonal cut

5 ribbon attatched

sew in place

A CAPE FOR A SUPERHERO

Turn your child into SuperKid by creating this fantastic cape from an old skirt or sheet. You can use any fabric you have at home, though don't use very heavy fabric as this might impede their flight. If you join smaller pieces of fabric, try and keep the seams vertical, as this will keep the fluid nature of the cape intact.

This design doesn't close around the child's neck, which can be very dangerous. Instead, it fastens under the arms and around the back. Keep the ties soft and loose, so that your superhero will be comfortable. To make sure you have enough fabric for the job, measure from your child's* shoulders to their ankles.

You will need

A piece of fabric the height of your child x 1500mm in a super colour

A button

*It's OK if you insert '28-year-old-friend' instead of 'child'. Everyone deserves to be super!

To make

1. Measure across your child's shoulders. Lay your fabric on a table and fold in half lengthways. From the fold, mark the width of your child's shoulders across the top. Cut the fabric diagonally to the bottom corner from this mark, cutting through both layers of fabric.

2. Hem the two diagonal sides and the bottom, by folding over the edges 15mm; press and pin in place. Sew these down and repeat to hide the raw edge.

3. Measure the length of tie needed by measuring from the centre of your child's back, under their left arm, across their shoulders, under their right arm and back to the centre. Add another 150mm for the join.

1

Super Kid

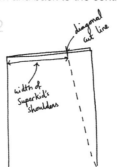

2

diagonal cut line

width of Superkid's shoulders

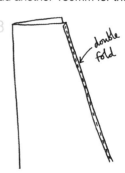

3

double fold

4&5

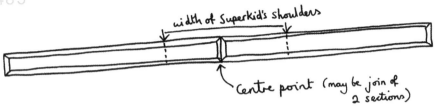

width of Superkid's shoulders

Centre point (may be join of 2 sections)

6&7

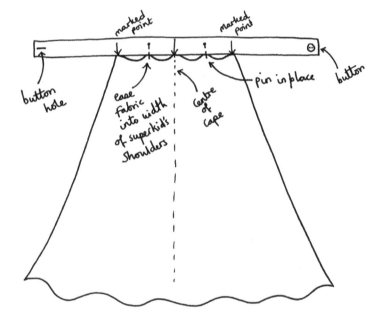

marked point

marked point

button hole

ease fabric into width of superkid's shoulders

centre of cape

pin in place

button

4. Cut a piece from the remaining fabric, measuring 150mm x the length measured. You may need to sew two sections together to get the required length.

5. Fold over the short sides of your tie 15mm, pin and sew down. Carefully fold in the long lengths 15mm, pressing as you go. Sew this down to create a neat hem. Fold the tie in half and find the centre. On each side of this point, mark off where your child's shoulders will fall.

6. Find the centre of the top edge of your cape and pin the centre of the tie in place as shown. Pin the right edge of the cape at the right marked point, and the left likewise. Gather the remaining fabric and pin to the tie as shown on page 57. Fold the tie over the raw edge and catch in the pins. Sew this down, continuing along both lengths of the tie.

7. Sew on a button at one end of the tie and make a hole at the other end, as shown on page 75. You may want to sew on a couple of buttons, so that your child can make the tie larger as they grow.

making jewellery

It's surprisingly easy to create fabric jewellery with a highly professional finish, especially if you use a mixture of fabric, buttons and found items. Heavy fabrics that don't fray easily are your friends when making jewellery – felt, or heavy woollen fabrics used for suits and coats. You will find that some designs for appliqué almost make a brooch in their own right, so why not simply sew a safety pin to the back and enjoy wearing it?

BROOCHES

These can be as large or as small as you want. We have made up a range of designs for you to try, all of them achieved through appliqué or by sewing on a button. A piece of graph paper will give you a good grid to sketch your designs on to. Again, if you work on a thicker fabric that doesn't fray, you won't need to hem around the perimeter.

When you have finished your design, simply cut out a second piece of fabric the same size or slightly smaller than your brooch design. Choose a safety pin to fit your brooch and cut a strip of fabric that will fit through the gap. This strip should be no longer than 40mm (or less, if your brooch is smaller).

Feed the strip through the pin and sew below and above the pin, as close as possible to the pin. This will secure it in place.   Sew the strip to the back section and then sew the back section to the brooch design, either by oversewing the edge with tiny stitches or simply machining a line around the perimeter.

BACK   FRONT

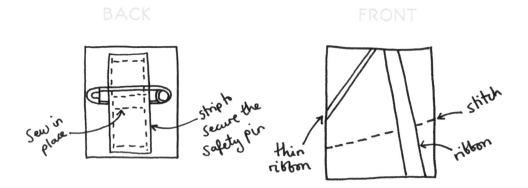

Sew in place — strip to secure the safety pin

thin ribbon

stitch

ribbon

METHUEN'S
ENGLISH CLASSICS

This brooch was made by Suzanne Harulow, more of which are available on her website.

CUFFS

These give you a wonderful opportunity to unleash your creativity and wear it on your sleeve. Cuffs are so easy to create and make fantastic gifts, even for those "difficult to buy for" teenage boys. Cuffs are best produced in a fairly thick fabric, though you can overcome the problem of thin fabric with a layer of interfacing.

Cuffs should be made to measure. As a rule, keep them to 200mm long and adjust them to fit the wearer. As with most items in this book, it's best to decorate the cuff before sewing it up, so decide on your design before you start. We have produced a number of options you can choose from.

If your backing fabric is thick, simply add a button and a hole to close. If you have chosen a thinner fabric, just fold in the sides, press flat and sew to another piece of fabric, keeping right sides out.

Fastening your cuffs

There are a number of options for fastening your cuffs; your choice will be dictated by your design. You could try sewing a small zip to your cuff, following the instructions on page 71, or a decorative button with matching hole (see page 75 for instructions). Alternatively, a discreet strip of Velcro will give you easy access, sewn to the corresponding sections. You could also make an unusual fastening with a piece of self-adhesive magnetic strip, secured in strategic places with a couple of stitches. This is available from most craft or hobby shops, and will be quite popular with younger recipients.

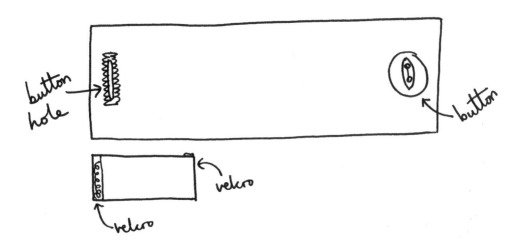

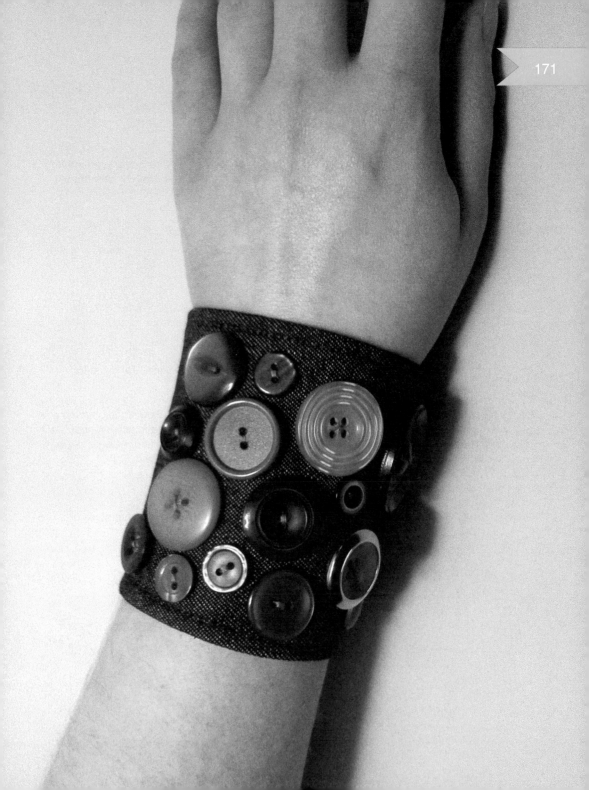

NECKLACES

Again, your appliqué designs can easily be threaded onto a piece of linen cord or a leather thong and, hey presto, you have a necklace. There are a million possibilities for this, but here are a couple of easier favourites.

T-SHIRT PLAIT

This is a lovely way of using up stained T-shirts and you can mix the plait with old costume jewellery chains or ribbon for a different effect. There is no sewing involved, just a little knot at the back to secure. This makes a great project for younger girls to tackle. You can use any colour T-shirt you like.

You will need

2 T-shirts

Ribbon

Costume chain
(optional)

To make

1. Cut the T-shirts into strips measuring 30mm wide. Tie the strips together to give you a length of 1000mm.

2. If you are plaiting in an old chain, open it out. Remember that the plait reduces the length of the chain, so you will need to use a longer chain. Begin plaiting together the T-shirt, chain and ribbon. You may wish to tape the ends to a table to make this easier.

3. Continue to plait until the necklace is finished.

4. Tie the ends together. If you wish, you can use another piece of T-shirt to wrap over the knot as shown.

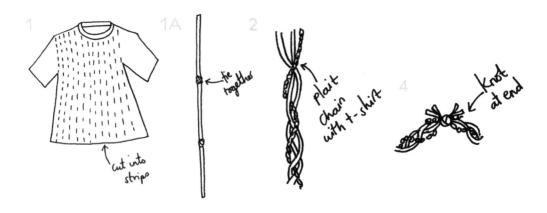

1

1A   ← tie together

2   plait chain with t-shirt

4   ← knot at end

cut into strips

Notes and Ideas

Larger stores

Abakhan
A one-stop shop for fabrics, craft supplies and knitting, they have stores all over the UK, each one with an excellent cheap rolls section. To find your local store, visit their website:
http://www.abakhan.co.uk/
Michael Abakhan Ltd, Coast Road, Llanerch-Y-Mor, Mostyn, Flintshire, CH8 9DX
01745 562 100

Fabric Warehouse
14 stores nationwide
www.fabricwarehouse.co.uk

HobbyCraft
www.hobbycraft.co.uk/

The Fabric Store
Six stores
www.thefabricstoreuk.co.uk/

Avon
Country Threads
2 Pierrepont Place, Bath,
Avon BA1 1JX
01225 480056

Bedfordshire
Singer Sewing Centre
www.singersewingcentre.moonfruit.com/
2A Lurke Street,
Bedford MK40 3HY
01234 350186

Tudor Rose Patchwork
www.tudorrosepatchwork.co.uk
The Garage, Station Road, Oakley,
Bedford MK43 7RB
01234 824983

Buckinghamshire
Worn and Washed Fabrics
www.wornandwashedfabrics.com
The Walled Garden, East Street, Olney,
Buckinghamshire MK46 4DW
01234 240881

Cambridgeshire
Top Stitch Fabrics
www.topstitchfabrics.co.uk
6 Hill Street, Wisbech,
Cambridgeshire PE13 1JX
01945 585828

Cheshire
TP Textiles
www.tptextiles.co.uk
53 Kingsway South,
Warrington WA4 1LQ
01925 242930

Cornwall
The Cotton Mills
www.cotton-mills.co.uk
Cotton Mills, Peoples Palace,
Truro TR1 2AZ
01872 278545

Truro Fabrics
www.trurofabrics.com
Lemon Quay, Truro,
Cornwall TR1 2LW
01872 222130

Cumbria
Fun 2 Do
www.fun2do.co.uk
21 Scotch Street, Carlisle,
Cumbria CA3 8PY
01228 523843

Derbyshire

Economy Fabrics
www.economy-fabrics.co.uk
44 Heath Road, Holmewood, Chesterfield,
Derbyshire S42 5RA
01246 855155

Patchwork Direct
www.patchworkdirect.com
Wesleyan House, Darley Dale,
Derbyshire DE4 2HX
01629 734100

Devon

Hulu
www.hulucrafts.co.uk
Sentinel House, Poundwell, Modbury,
Devon PL21 0XX
01548 831911

Meme Fabric Shop
www.memefabrics.co.uk
1 Upper Paul Street, Exeter, Devon EX4 3NB
01392 438578

Percy's Fabrics & Haberdashery Ltd
33 Sidwell Street,
Exeter EX4 6NS
01392 412314

Sew Bazaar
www.sewbazaar.co.uk
20 North Street,
Exeter EX4 3QS
01392 428105

Tavy Textiles
www.tavytextiles.co.uk
1–2 Bank Square,
Tavistock PL19 0DE
01822 613994

Dorset

So 'N' Sews
www.sonsews.co.uk
24 Westham Road, Weymouth,
Dorset DT4 8NU
01305 766411

Zebedee Fabrics
120–124 Seabourne Road, Bournemouth,
Dorset BH5 2HY
01202 422811

Essex

Just Fabrics
102 High Street,
Maldon CM9 5ET
01621 852552

The Cheap Shop
www.thecheapshop.ltd.uk
108 Church Road, Tiptree, Colchester,
Essex CO5 0AB
01621 815576

The Remnant Shop
www.fabric8online.co.uk
12 Head Street, Colchester, Essex CO1 1NY
01206 763432

Gloucestershire

Beckford Silk
www.beckfordsilk.co.uk
Beckford, Nr Tewksbury,
Gloucestershire GL20 7AU
01386 881507

Painswick Fabrics
www.painswickfabrics.co.uk
New Street, Painswick,
Gloucestershire GL6 6XH
01452 812616

Hampshire
Cutting Edge Fabrics
Brighton Hill Centre, Brighton Hill Parade,
Basingstoke RG22 4EH

C&H Fabrics Ltd
www.candh.co.uk
7–8 High Street, Winchester SO23 9JX
01962 843355

Herefordshire
Doughtys
www.doughtysonline.co.uk
Haberdashery 33 Church Street,
Hereford HR1 2LR
01432 352546
Fabrics: 3 Capuchin Yard, Off Church Street,
Hereford HR1 2LR
01432 265561

Fabric Mills
www.fabricmills.co.uk
120–122 Monnow Street,
Monmouth NP25 3EQ
01600 775531

Hertfordshire
Fashion Fabrics
www.fashion-n-fabrics.com
24 Beech Road, St Albans,
Hertfordshire AL3 5AS
01727 865038

Zips N Clips
www.zipsnclips.co.uk
92B Haldens, Welwyn Garden City,
Hertfordshire AL7 1DD
01707 331777

Kent
Fabric & Woodcraft Centre Ltd
90 Featherby Road, Gillingham ME8 6AW
01634 231366

Just Fabrics
www.justfabrics.uk.com
The Pentagon, Chatham ME4 4HW
01634 827063

Rainham Sewing Centre
12 Station Road, Rainham,
Gillingham ME8 7PH
01634 233243

The Fabric Shop
46A Harbour Street, Whitstable CT5 1AH
01227 273272

Lancashire
Clark Craft Products
www.clarkcraft.co.uk
Empire Works, Railway Street, Ramsbottom,
Bury, Lancashire BL0 9AS
08000 371420

Fine Fabrics Burnley
www.finefabrics-burnley.co.uk
Oakmount Mill, Wiseman Street, Burnley,
Lancashire BB11 1RU
01282 414950

Lords Sewing
www.lordsewing.co.uk
Oswaldtwistle Mills, Colliers Street,
Oswaldtwistle, Lancashire BB5 3DE
01254 389171

Nortex Mill Factory Shop Ltd
www.nortexmill.co.uk
105 Chorley Old Road, Bolton BL1 3AS
01204 844907

Leicestershire

Direct Fabric Warehouse
www.directfabric.co.uk
Lee Circle, Lee Street, Leicester LE1 3RE
0116 251 242

Vend Fabrics
www.vendfabricsonline.co.uk
Vend Fabrics Ltd, 25 Charter Street,
Leicester LE1 3UD
0116 253 0225

Lincolnshire

Grimsby Sewing and Knitting
www.grimsbysewingandknitting.co.uk
216 Freeman Street, Grimsby, North East
Lincolnshire DN32 9DR
01472 343921

Tetford Fabrics Mail Order Only
www.tetfordfabrics.co.uk
Tetford Fabrics, Rosedale, West Road, Tetford,
Horncastle, Lincolnshire LN9 6QP
01507 533682

London

Borovick Fabrics
www.borovickfabricsltd.co.uk
16 Berwick Street, London W1F 0HP
020 7437 2180

Fabrics Galore
www.fabricsgalore.co.uk
52–54 Lavender Hill, London SW11 5RH
020 7738 9589

Manchester

Fred Aldous
www.fredaldous.co.uk
37 Lever Street, Northern Quarter,
Manchester M1 1LW
0161 236 4224

Norfolk

Anglian Fashion Fabrics
www.anglianfashionfabrics.co.uk
29 Magdalen Street, Norwich NR3 1LE
01603 611661

The Fabric Shop
Reepham Road, Norwich, Norfolk NR6 5PA
01603 413017

Northamptonshire

Mrs Sew N Sew
www.mrssew-n-sew.co.uk
57A Haines Road, Far Cotton, Northampton,
Northamptonshire NN4 8DS
01604 432119

Poppy Patch
www.poppypatch.co.uk
3 Manor Farm Court, Church Lane, Great
Doddington, Northamptonshire NN29 7TR
01933 227973

Northumberland

Absolutely Fabrics
www.absolutelyfabricsuk.com/
20c North Tyne Industrial Estate, Benton,
Newcastle upon Tyne
NE12 9SZ
0191 266 2070

1st For Fabrics
www.1stforfabrics.co.uk
Unit 20, J&H North Tyne Industrial Estate
Whitley Road,
Newcastle upon Tyne NE12 9SZ
0191 270 1333

Factory Fabrics
www.factoryfabriccentre.co.uk/
Factory Fabrics, Prudhoe, Textile House, Princess
Way, Prudhoe, Northumberland NE42 6HD
01661 836717

Nottinghamshire

Millcroft Textiles
www.millcrofttextiles.co.uk
Stewart House, Catton Road, Arnold,
Nottingham NG5 7JD
0115 953 2182

My Fabric Place
www.myfabricplace.co.uk
12 High Road, Chilwell, Beeston,
Nottingham NG9 4AE
0115 943 6636

Oxfordshire

Freelance Fabrics
www.freelancefabrics.com
4 High Street, Kidlington OX5 2DL
01865 841088

Just Fabrics
www.justfabrics.co.uk
Cheltenham Road, Burford,
Oxfordshire OX18 4JA
01993 823391

Village Fabrics
www.villagefabrics.co.uk
4–5 Saint Leonards Square,
Wallingford, OX10 0AS
01491 204100

Shropshire

Dunelm Fabric Shop
Bridge Road, Wellington,
Telford, TF1 1ED
01952 243440

Watson and Thornton
Fabrics and Haberdashery
www.watsonandthornton.co.uk/
27/28 Mardol, Shrewsbury,
Shropshire SY1 1PU
01743 236569

Somerset

Hansons Fabrics and Crafts
www.hansonsfabrics.co.uk
Hansons Fabrics, Station Road,
Sturminster Newton, Dorset DT10 1BD
01258 472698

Hoopers Ltd
25 High Street, Bridgwater TA6 3BG
01278 422586

Staffordshire

Pollyanna Patchwork
www.shop.pollyanna-patchwork.co.uk
12 High Street, Eccleshall,
Staffordshire ST21 6BZ
01785 859360

R.A.B. Fabrics
5 The Strand, Stoke-on-Trent ST3 2JF
01782 310661

Suffolk

Quilters Haven
www.quilters-haven.co.uk
68 High Street, Wickham Market,
Suffolk IP13 0QU
01728 746275

Sew Creative
www.sewcreative.co.uk
23 Hatter Street,
Bury St Edmunds IP33 1NE
01284 755459

Surrey

Creative Quilting
www.creativequilting.co.uk
30–32 Bridge Road,
East Molesey KT8 9HA
020 8941 7075

Mitchell Fabrics
18 Bridge Street,
Godalming GU7 1HY
01483 411900

The Quilt Room
www.quiltroom.co.uk
37/39 High Street, Dorking,
Surrey RH4 1AR
01306 877307

Sussex

Ditto Fabrics
21 Kensington Gardens, Brighton,
East Sussex BN1 4AL
01273 603771

Fabric Land
www.fabricland.co.uk
76 Western Road, Brighton,
East Sussex BN1 2HA
01273 822257

The Stitchery (Lewes) Ltd
www.the-stitchery.co.uk
12–14 Riverside, Cliffe Bridge, High Street,
Lewes BN7 2RE
01273 473 577

Warwickshire

Decorative Cloth
www.decorativecloth.com
122 Warwick Street, Leamington Spa,
Warwickshire CV32 4QY
01926 312679

Royal Fabrics and Haberdashery
4 Church Walk, Leamington Spa
Warwickshire CV31 1EF
01926 425628

West Midlands

Barry's Fabric Superstore
1 Moseley Street, Birmingham, West Midlands
B5 6JX
0121 622 6102

The Cotton Patch
www.cottonpatch.co.uk
The Cotton Patch
1283–1285 Stratford Road, Hall Green,
Birmingham B28 9AJ
0121 702 2840

Wiltshire

Fabric Magic
www.fabricmagic.co.uk
14 Silver Street, Trowbridge, Wiltshire BA14
8AE
01225 768833

Phase Patch
www.phasepatch.co.uk
1 Causeway, Chippenham, Wiltshire SN15 3BT
01249 655511

Worcester

Fabrik Shop
24A Broad Street, Pershore,
Worcestershire WR10 1AY
01386 553626

Rags
Crowngate Shopping Centre, Chapel Walk,
Town Centre, Worcester WR1 3LD
01905 612330

Yorkshire

Gillies Fabrics
www.gilliesfabricsyork.co.uk
2 Peter Lane, York YO1 8SW
01904 626244

ISH Ltd
www.ishfabrics.com
400–402 Sharrow Vale Road, Sheffield, South
Yorkshire S11 8ZP
0114 267 1964

Samuel Taylor
www.clickoncrafts.co.uk
10 Central Road, Leeds, West Yorkshire LS1
6DE
0113 245 9737

Waltons Mill Shop Harrogate
www.waltonsmillshopharrogate.co.uk
41 Tower Street, Harrogate HG1 1HS
01423 225429

Northern Ireland

Craftworld
www.craft-world.co.uk
23-29 Queen Street, Belfast BT1 6EA
02890249000

Mitchells
124 Longstone Street, Lisburn,
County Antrim BT28 1TR
028 9267 7946

Mrs Sew 'N' Sew
14 Mandeville St, Craigavon,
County Armagh BT62 3NZ
028 3833 6567

The Patchwork Goose
34 Antrim Rd, Belfast,
County Antrim BT15 2HF
028 9035 1465

Quilters Quest
www.quiltersquest.co.uk
361 Woodstock Road,
Belfast BT6 8PU
028 90454745

Scotland

Allan's Haberdashery
29 High St, Fochabers,
Morayshire IV32 7DX
01343 820238

The Grassmarket Embroidery Shop
19 Grassmarket, Old Town,
Edinburgh EH1 2HS
0131 226 3335

Helens Haberdashery
Unit 61 Forge Shopping Centre,
1221 Gallowgate
Glasgow G31 4EB

The Needle Point
14 West Port, Selkirk,
Selkirkshire TD7 4DG

The Sewing Basket
www.sewing-basket.co.uk/
61 Newmarket Street,
Ayr KA7 1LL
01292 261841

Wales

Betty's Fabrics
www.bettysfabrics.co.uk
1 Mostyn Broadway
Llandudno LL30 1YL
01492 877282

Isabeau Inspirations
www.isabeau-inspirations.co.uk
Crosshand Square Shopping Centre
Pontardulais Road, Cross Hands
Llanelli SA14 6NT
01269 844969

Janes of Fishguard
www.janes-fishguard.co.uk
14-18 High Street, Fishguard,
Pembrokeshire SA65 9AR
01348 874443

Knitandsew
www.knitandsew.co.uk
21/22 Park Street,
Swansea SA1 3DJ
0845 0940835

Nantiago
www.sewingnantiago.co.uk
3 White Horse Lane, Abergavenny,
Monmouthshire NP7 5AS
01873 854091

Websites

www.online-fabrics.co.uk

www.endoflinefabrics.co.uk

www.paperthreadfabrics

www.castleandthings.com.au

www.crushculdesac.tumblr.com

www.lilysquilts.blogspot.com

www.freespiritfabric.com

www.justeleanor.com/portfolio

www.valoriwells.com

www.lulisanchez.com

www.katiemoth.co.uk

www.georgiacoote.co.uk

www.sharonblackman.co.uk

www.dyermakerstudio.com

www.alicepotter.co.uk

www.poppytreffry.co.uk

www.kanganarora.blogspot.com

www.blog.kiranravilious.com

www.husandhem.co.uk/9-furnishings-and-fabrics

www.dwell.com

www.designsponge.com

Textile designers who have helped us

Lu Summers
www.lusummers.co.uk

Georgia Coote
www.georgiacoote.co.uk

Suzanne Harulow
www.skybluesea.co.uk

Thank you!

We would like to thank everyone who helped with the making of this book, especially Suzanne Harulow for her gorgeous work, Lu Summers and Georgia Coote for the kind donation of their beautiful fabrics and Abakhan Fabrics for their huge bag of scraps.

About us

Rebecca Peacock and Sam Tickner are the founders of Firecatcher, a creative company that specialises in illustration and design. They have been sewing for years, from specially bound books, to personalised bags, to sewn elements for illustration. You can see more of their work by visiting their website: **www.firecatcher.co.uk**

The make and mend blog

You can find more patterns, projects and inspirational items by visiting our blog: makeandmendbook.blogspot.com, created specially for this book. Send us your pictures, projects and ideas and we'll post them on the blog to share with the Make and Mend community.

Notes and Ideas

Index